✳ attract birds to your garden

essentials

joe firmin

Foulsham
LONDON • NEW YORK • TORONTO • SYDNEY

foulsham

The Publishing House, Bennetts Close, Cippenham, Slough, Berkshire, SL1 5AP, England

ISBN 0-572-02798-2

Cover photograph © Ardea London/Brian Bevan

Illustrations of the stock dove, swift, rook, yellowhammer, carrion crow, black-headed gull, waxwing and feral pigeon by Michael Stringer.

Printed in Great Britain by Creative Print and Design Wales, Ebbw Vale

Contents

Introduction

In these days of increased leisure and a growing interest in the garden as a place for relaxation and pleasure, many people want to make their gardens attractive to birds. There is a great advantage in feeding birds in the garden during those months of the year when there is only a minimum of natural food. Many people with gardens are also interested in providing nest boxes and natural cover suitable for nesting.

Adaptable creatures like birds are certainly not discouraged by built-up areas, and those new to birdwatching will be surprised by the number and variety of birds they can encourage into their garden. If you provide their basic requirements they will feed happily and even nest quite close to the house. Many of the most common birds adapted their lives to our gardens after their original woodland and hedgerow homes had been either destroyed or modified through human activities. They then found that the closeness of people protected them from such natural enemies as the fox, weasel, stoat and wild cat on the ground, and birds of prey, magpies and crows in the air. Swallows, house martins, house sparrows and starlings found human homes gave them plenty of places in which to nest and rear their young.

The aim of this book is to help you learn more about the birds that already live in or near your garden, and also how to encourage different species to visit. It includes a comprehensive identification guide to the most common species, with superb full-colour artwork so that you can identify the birds easily. It gives you advice not only on suitable foods for the various species, but also on how to give that food to the birds, as it will tell you how to choose and position a bird table, and even how to make one yourself. Encouraging birds to nest in your garden will also increase the numbers you attract, and there is full information on making and placing nest boxes.

Bird tables, bird feeders and nest boxes can give you endless pleasure from watching the lively behaviour and colourful plumage of the surprisingly large variety of birds that visit even the smallest gardens. Once you have begun to enjoy your birdwatching, you can use the later chapters of the book to help you create a miniature bird sanctuary in your garden, planting or encouraging the most bird-friendly plants in a design that will help the birds find food, nesting materials and locations, perches and roosts.

Even those who are without a garden, or unable to go out of doors because of illness or infirmity, can still derive a great deal of enjoyment from a bird-feeding station on a window-sill. Low-cost, low-maintenance and easy to install, this is also an excellent option for those in flats and apartments.

One of my friends is a retired army officer who is almost

completely bed-ridden, but he keeps cheerful and busy watching birds and keeping a record of those that visit. He has clamped a bird table to a wide window-sill outside his bedroom and hangs from it a variety of wire or nylon containers, and baskets containing nuts and household scraps. He has already listed some uncommon species. As well as blue tits, great tits, coal tits and greenfinches, the regular visitors, his greatest triumph so far has been to attract some siskins, pretty green and yellow finches, to his red nylon peanut bags. These little birds, winter visitors from northern Britain, cling acrobatically to the bags as they peck at the nuts through the mesh.

Hopefully, the information in this little book will help you to encourage a variety of beautiful birds into your garden, and give you enough information to learn more about them and their habits. And an added bonus is that the gardener who sets out to attract and protect birds is playing a part in the conservation of our precious wildlife.

Chapter 1
Feeding Habits and Suitable Foods

P roviding birds with appropriate food and water is the simplest way to encourage them into your garden so, in this first chapter, we are going to look at the feeding preferences of the most common birds, as well as what and when to feed. It takes very little effort to get into the routine of feeding the birds, and you will be rewarded so quickly by new and fascinating visitors – once they have become used to the fact that they can rely on you as a food source – that you will wonder why you did not start feeding the birds years earlier.

Feeding preferences

Before you start to think about supplying the birds with food, it is important to know a little about what is best for them, and when you should feed them. If you take a close look at the beaks of the various species – both in these illustrations and by looking at the birds in your garden – you will see that their shape is clearly indicative of the feeding habits of those particular birds and therefore the foods they prefer.

Finches, tits and sparrows have strong, stubby bills adapted to crush seeds and grains.

Hawfinch   Great Tit

Robins, thrushes, wrens, dunnocks and warblers have slender bills that they use for feeding on insects and other soft-bodied creatures.

Robin   Song Thrush

The woodpecker's long, powerful bill is ideal for probing into the crevices of tree bark, while the nuthatch uses its slender, strong bill to wedge seeds into crevices, then crack them open.

Woodpecker   Nuthatch

By observing the birds and their bills, you will soon be able to judge the sort of foods they are adapted for, even if you have never noticed that type of bird before.

Bird-seed mixtures

There is a whole range of ready-made wild bird food mixtures on the market, and the best of these have been specially formulated to satisfy the appetites and nutritional needs of a wide variety of birds. The downside is that they are fairly expensive and you will need a lot during the winter months, so to start with you might like to supplement proprietary mixtures by adding flaked maize, millet, dry oatmeal, sunflower seeds, or other wild or garden seeds you have gathered and dried.

Once you are in the habit of feeding the birds, however, you may want to be a bit more adventurous in what you feed your garden visitors.

Natural foods

As you would expect, the best foods for birds are those they would normally find in their natural habitat. If you have a mixture of trees and shrubs in your garden that produce edible berries and fruits, and herbaceous plants with nutritious seeds, you are already a long way towards ensuring plenty of suitable food for the birds in autumn and winter. (We'll go into more detail on the best plants to cultivate in Chapter 4.)

You can supplement the seeds and berries that the birds find naturally in your garden by going into the countryside in late summer and autumn to gather berries from the rowan, elder and hawthorn, as well as hazel nuts and acorns. Spread out the berries to dry first, then store them in a cool place out of strong sunlight, and they will keep for a long time. Acorns and hazel nuts can be stored almost indefinitely as long as they are kept dry. You can also gather fir, pine and larch cones and take out the seeds from their scales to feed your birds.

I make a point of picking the seed heads of wild plants such as dock, thistle, stinging nettle, knapweed, teasel and ragwort. I place them in muslin bags and hang them up until they have dried out completely, then I shake or beat out the dry, clean seeds when they are needed for the bird table. Sometimes, I also add the seeds of wild or garden plants to packet seed mixtures. Where I live, in the countryside, I can sometimes buy bags of the cleanings from the machines of seed merchants or farmers. These contain a mixture of weed seeds and grain that make ideal bird food, although you must make sure that they are free from chemical dressings or pollutants.

Almost any kind of nut is good for the birds. Peanuts are the first choice, rich in calories and easy to handle and store. They are readily available to buy loose, either shelled or in their shells, and quite inexpensive. Remember that you must never feed salted peanuts, or any other salted nuts, to birds as this can cause them to become dehydrated.

If you do not remove the shells you can string some peanuts on stout thread to hang from the bird table or a branch. Tits and nuthatches adore swinging on these peanut strings, but they are not the only birds that like peanuts. Chaffinches and jays will carry away an endless supply, and whole nuts will also attract woodpeckers.

Peanut strings attract tits and nuthatches.

You can also wedge the kernels of almonds and brazil nuts into the crevices of posts or trellises to encourage nuthatches and woodpeckers to hammer with their bills to retrieve the nuts. Another idea is to hang shelled brazil nuts or almonds on string, or chop them and put them on the bird table.

Coconut is popular with many birds. Saw a shell in half and suspend the pieces upside down so that the rain cannot collect inside, and the tits and other small birds can hang on to the coconut and peck at the food inside. If you do hang a coconut with the cup uppermost, drill a hole through the base to allow rain water to drain out. Make sure you change the coconut regularly. Never offer desiccated (dried) or ground coconut; it swells up in the birds' stomachs with disastrous results.

Soft fruits are also suitable as bird food. If you collect crab apples, or have some leftover pears, bananas, grapes or apples, stack them carefully on trays to store them so that they do not bruise – otherwise they will rot – and the birds will thoroughly enjoy them.

Other foods

You can avoid any extra outlay by feeding your kitchen scraps to your garden birds. Bread is the most common waste, and wholemeal is more nourishing for the birds as well as for humans, although you should not put this out when nestlings are being fed in spring and summer as it is not the best food for them. Birds often prefer uncooked pastry to bread, so you do not need to waste your pastry trimmings. You can simply mould them into shapes to fit a corner of the bird table or feed tray. Potatoes baked in their jackets are popular, and birds also eagerly eat stale cake. You can put out flaked maize, millet, dry oatmeal or cooked rice. Make sure that cake and similar foods are not put on the bird table in wet weather, though, otherwise they will soon be reduced to a soggy, inedible mess.

Meat should always be cooked to avoid any danger of birds carrying off lumps of meat that could spread disease, but chopped pieces of cooked bacon rinds or other meats can be put out for the birds, as can chopped pieces of cheese or cheese rind. You can also hang up pieces of bacon rind in strips on a wire or stout cord. Fat can be used to bind together bird puddings (see below), but you can also pour it into meshed containers then leave it to set, or stuff it into the small round holes bored in a suet stick – a short length of silver birch log which can then be hung from a tree or the bird table (see page 26). This provides hours of entertainment for the birdwatcher as well as food for tits, and even woodpeckers and nuthatches. Tits also love lumps of beef suet, tied on a string, on which they can swing as they pick off lumps.

Making a meal of scraps

You can use a variety of ingredients to make a pudding to feed to the birds, using whatever you have to hand, but avoid any salty or spicy foods as these are not suitable. Put some seeds, peanuts, oatmeal, chopped cheese, chopped bacon rind, dry cake and other scraps into a container and weigh it roughly. Melt half the weight of fat, pour it over the mixture and leave it to set. Once it has hardened, you can turn the pudding out on to the bird table or, if you insert a hook into the base of the pudding before you make it, you can hang it from a tree or the bird table (see page 37).

Live food

Mealworms are the best kind of live food for birds, but you can also offer ants' eggs (actually the pupae, not the eggs, of ants) and gentles (fly grubs). You can buy gentles from fishing tackle and bait shops. Ants' eggs can be gathered from wild nests or you can buy them from pet shops or dealers in aquaria.

Personally I much prefer mealworms to gentles, however, as gentles are bad for nestlings. You can buy supplies of mealworms, the larvae of a small black beetle, from pet shops and put them out on the bird table or a ledge in a glazed china dish. Robins are crazy about them and, with a little patience, you can easily tame one to come and take them from your hand.

If you want to try your hand at producing your own mealworms, buy about 300 from a pet shop. Punch some ventilation holes in the lid of a large biscuit tin and line the bottom of the tin with three layers of hessian, each one sprinkled with pieces of wholemeal bread, bran, pieces of raw potato and some of the mealworms, and keep them in a warm place. The mealworms go in and out of the hessian and eat the food. After a few weeks, they turn into pupae from which adult beetles eventually emerge. These pair up and produce eggs, renewing the supply of mealworms.

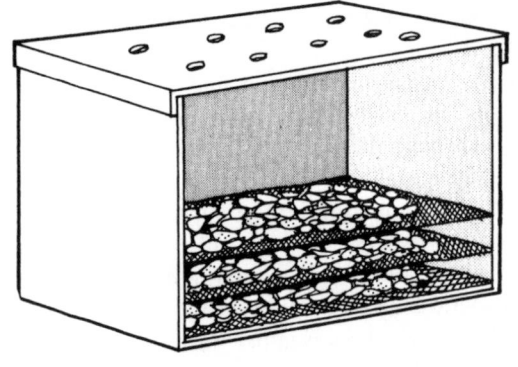

You can produce your own mealworms in a specially adapted biscuit tin.

When and how much to feed

Birds should be fed regularly at the same time each day. They depend on you for survival in the worst of the winter weather and will soon become accustomed to your garden as a source of food. If the weather is very harsh, the less energy they need to expend searching for food the better.

It is important to put out no more food than can be

consumed before nightfall, in order to avoid encouraging rats and mice into the garden to finish off what is left. You therefore need to judge how much food to put out depending on how many birds visit your garden. If you over-estimate and there is food left at the end of the day, sweep away any crumbs and food residue from the bird table or feeding station so that it does not collect there.

Through the spring, summer and autumn, there is ample natural food available for the birds, so you should really only feed them through the late autumn and winter. Start as soon as the temperatures fall sharply and supplies of natural foods begin to decline. As a general rule, feeding the birds in the garden is most valuable when the harder weather sets in at the end of the year and throughout the bleak months of January and February. This is the vital time for bird survival.

Stop feeding when the weather warms up in the early spring, by which time there is an increasing amount of insect life and other natural foods so birds will be disinclined to visit the bird table anyway. Recent springs have been late and cold so the time for stopping supplies of home-made or proprietary bird foods must be a matter of common sense, taking into account the prevailing weather conditions. As soon as there is consistently warm weather, stop feeding.

It is also important to remember especially that nuts and other high-protein or soft and sticky foods offered on bird tables and in containers can be harmful if fed to young nestlings.

Peanuts, for example, cannot be properly digested by nestling tits even though their parents eat and enjoy the nuts, so discontinue these foods during the nesting season.

You can maintain interest in the bird table through spring, summer and early autumn by making regular, small offerings of low-bulk foods. If you feel you want to keep some peanuts out for the adult birds during the spring and summer, make sure they are in a small-mesh container so the birds can only peck at them, as large pieces could also choke the young.

Where to feed

We have already established that different birds have different feeding habits, so you may want to put out your bird food in several places in the garden to suit a variety of species.

Your bird table is likely to be the focus of activity, and you should position this near enough to a perch on a tree or shrub, but not too close to conceal predators. Peanuts or other foods can be hung from beneath the bird table or from trees or trellises.

Some birds do not like to feed at a bird table. You can cater for their needs by putting out food on an old tray or a piece of board that is left on the ground under a tree or between shrubs, though again not too close to any cover from which a lurking cat could pounce. Dunnocks, chaffinches, yellowhammers, and even blackbirds and song thrushes, seem to prefer feeding on the ground to jostling with other birds on a table.

One of the great attractions of some garden birds is their tameness. However, you should bear in mind that birds like the jackdaw and starling, which quickly lose their fear of humans when offered food, can take most of the supplies you provide for shyer species. You will certainly see a definite pecking order on your bird table. Carefully selecting the foods you put out to appeal to specific species can help to encourage the smaller birds.

When a number of birds are attracted into an area to feed, the dangers of disease increases. It is therefore essential that you check tables and any feeding areas regularly and sweep them clear to ensure that there is no build-up of food particles. Occasionally scrub bird tables and containers using a 10 per cent disinfectant solution, then rinse them with clean water to get rid of any chemical residue.

Hand feeding

Robins are easy to tame and even to encourage to take food from your hand. You will need to offer food regularly at the same place, and be prepared to be very patient while the bird gets used to your presence. Robins are delightful to have near the house, but a tame robin is often more aggressive than one that is treated like the other birds in the garden. He tends to be lord of the bird table or window-sill. So if you train a robin to take food from your hand, it is better to do it on the opposite side of the house from the bird table.

Water

As well as food, birds need a constant supply of water both for drinking and to keep their plumage in top condition. After a bath, a bird rubs its feathers with oil collected from the preen gland above its tail. Birds love to bathe in summer and winter alike and the cold does not worry them – starlings will even break the ice on a bird bath to bathe in the depths of winter.

Unless you have a pond or stream in your garden, you must turn your attention to supplying water for the birds from another source, although if you are really keen on establishing the bird garden, you may want to create your own pond (see page 73).

You can buy bird baths and there is a huge variety available at pet shops and garden centres. The best are expensive, but you may decide to add one to your Christmas or birthday list! A simple and much cheaper alternative is to use an upturned dustbin lid, either sunk in the ground or supported on three bricks. The depth of the water should be not more than 10 cm (4 in). Make sure it is clean and free from any pollutants.

If you have time, you can look round junk shops or attend auctions for one of those solidly made Victorian metal saucer baths, which are easy to convert into a small pond or large bird bath. Sunk into the ground in a partly shaped spot with a layer of fine sand underneath the bottom, the bath can be planted with water weeds, rushes and water lilies.

Position your bird bath close to some trees or shrubs that the birds can use as a natural staging post before visiting the bird bath, but do not place it too near any shrubbery that may conceal a cat or other predator.

If the water freezes in winter, you need to melt it so that the birds can still drink or bathe. One useful tip in winter is to float a plastic ball in the water, then if the pond freezes you can lift it out to reveal an unfrozen circle and more easily melt the remaining ice with hot water. Or you can line your bird bath with a sheet of sturdy polythene so that the ice can be removed easily and you can refill the bath with water. Alternatively use hot water to melt the ice. Never use glycerine or other anti-freeze additives; they are injurious to birds' plumage. And remember, if your pond contains fish, do not break the ice with a heavy implement – the shock waves will kill the fish.

If you have a large bird bath you can prevent it from freezing by using an aquarium immersion heater covered with gravel. If it is connected to a submerged thermostat it will prevent a freeze-up. Make sure the mains lead is of outdoor quality and check all fittings to ensure your own safety and that of the birds. If there is anything you are not sure about, consult a qualified electrician. You can also put a slow-burning night lamp under a bird bath raised above ground.

Bird baths must be cleaned regularly as they soon build up a layer of algae, dead leaves and bird droppings. You can dilute household disinfectants (about a 10 per cent solution) to use to clean the bath, but make sure that you rinse out the bath thoroughly to remove any traces of chemicals before you refill it.

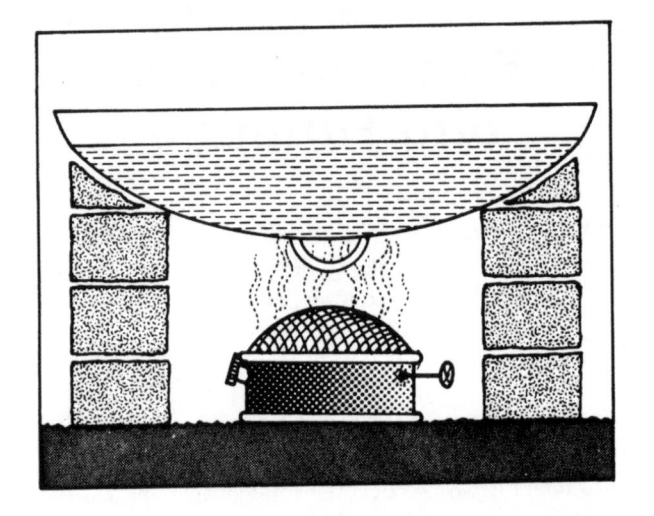

A slow-burning night lamp can be used to prevent a raised
bird bath from freezing.

Chapter 2
Bird Tables and Bird Furniture

There are many useful items of bird-garden furniture that you can buy or make to help to attract more birds into your garden, for example, tables, perches, feeders and nut dispensers. Correctly placed and maintained, they can all add to your enjoyment of birdwatching.

Bird tables

The main item of equipment for feeding birds in the garden is the bird table. It pays to devote as much time and cash as you can afford to buying or making a sturdy, weather-resistant model.

A good size for a bird table is about 30 × 45 cm (12 × 18 in), with a flat surface and a lip around the outside to prevent the food from sliding off. I prefer a table with a roof as it helps to keep the food dry and provides a place to hang a seed hopper. Birds also like somewhere to shelter from driving rain, sleet and snow, and will huddle under the bird table roof in severe weather. However, some people may tell you that they consider a roof unnecessary and contend that it serves to attract

A simple bird table is suitable for the smallest of gardens.

feathered and furred enemies that lurk under its cover or use it as a vantage point to launch attacks on the birds visiting the tables. I do not agree, but the choice is obviously yours.

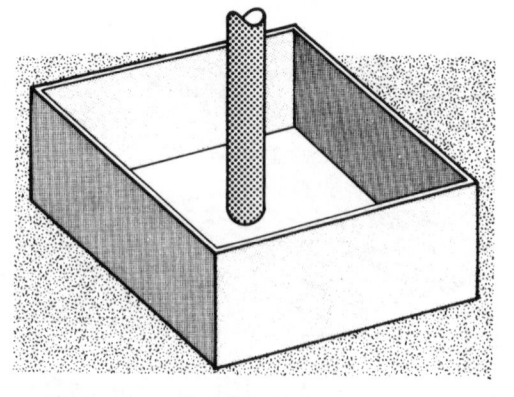

An open biscuit tin on the ground below a bird table will deter unwelcome animals.

You can either buy bird tables ready made or make your own. The Royal Society for the Protection of Birds makes and sells a standard bird table that I can strongly recommend. You will find details on page 202, together with information on other reputable suppliers of bird tables and general garden bird equipment.

There are many different styles, but steer clear of the curious rustic tables ornamented with all sorts of perches and roof adornments. The simpler and cleaner the table, the better it will function – and it will be less likely to attract unwelcome predators and pests.

You must fit your table to a smooth pole, which can be made of metal or wood. Rustic or rough-barked poles may look attractive, but they offer the perfect invitation to clambering cats and squirrels. As an anti-squirrel device, you can fit an old biscuit tin on the ground under the bird table. Simply place it on the ground, open-end up, and drive the pole through it. Leave the top of the tin open and no animal will climb over it.

One problem with a bird table is the dominant and aggressive behaviour of certain species, particularly starlings and house sparrows, which grab a lot of the food by sheer weight of

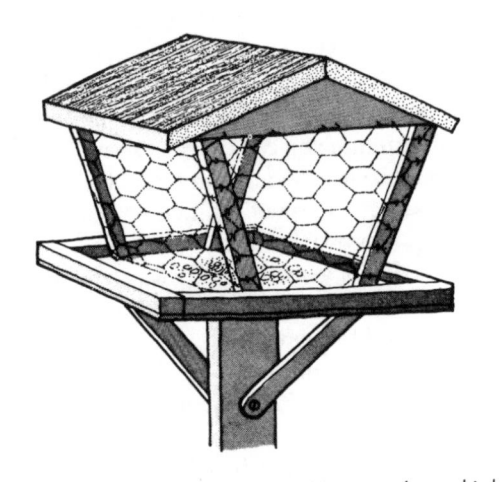

Wire mesh around the bird table will keep out larger birds.

numbers. In recent years, it has been the wood pigeon that has taken on the role of the bully at the bird table. One way of keeping them out and allowing other birds to have a greater share of the food on the bird table is to surround it with wire netting, with mesh wide enough to admit only small birds. The problem is that this method will also deter blackbirds and thrushes. I think the best option is to offer the pigeons food in an area of the garden separate from the main feeding stations, which allows other species a better chance of feeding at the bird table.

Making a bird table

If you are thinking of making your own table, it is worth bearing in mind that the cost of wood is extremely high and not likely to come down, but if you shop around or use wood salvaged from other pieces of furniture you can cut the expense.

If you do decide to make your own bird table, you should not make the feeding tray too small. Mine is 45 × 30 cm (18 × 12 in) but you can go for a larger area if you wish. Common sense dictates the size; do not get so carried away by your enthusiasm that you try to make a big, unwieldy tray that will frighten away the birds and be hard to support.

Include a simple roof and put a lip about 3 cm (1¼ in) high round the edge of the tray but leave a gap for easy cleaning of the table and drainage of rain water. The lip prevents food that has been scattered on the table from being blown away by the wind or swept off by scuffling birds. Pieces of bread or other

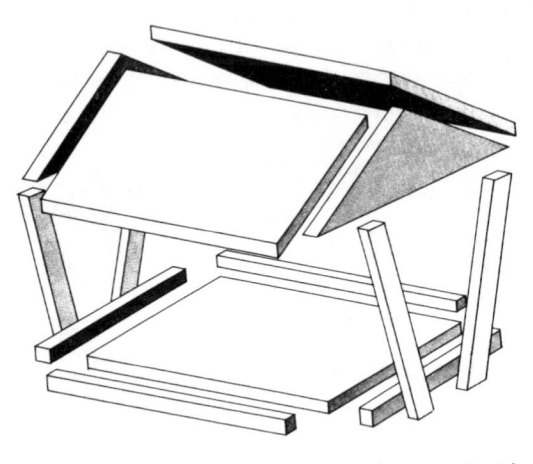

A good size for a bird table is about 45 x 30 cm (18 x 12 in) with a simple
roof and a ledge round the flat tray.

food can also be pushed against the ledge by birds to make
pecking and picking up easier.

Positioning your bird table

Siting your bird table in the best possible position is essential
both for the convenience and safety of the birds and so that you
can watch them from the best vantage point. Place the bird table
near the cover of some shrubs or a hedge so that the birds have
somewhere safe to perch before they alight on the table, but out

of range of an agile cat. Do not put it in the middle of a lawn where there is always the risk of interference from cats and squirrels or, in larger gardens, from owls and hawks. Birds do

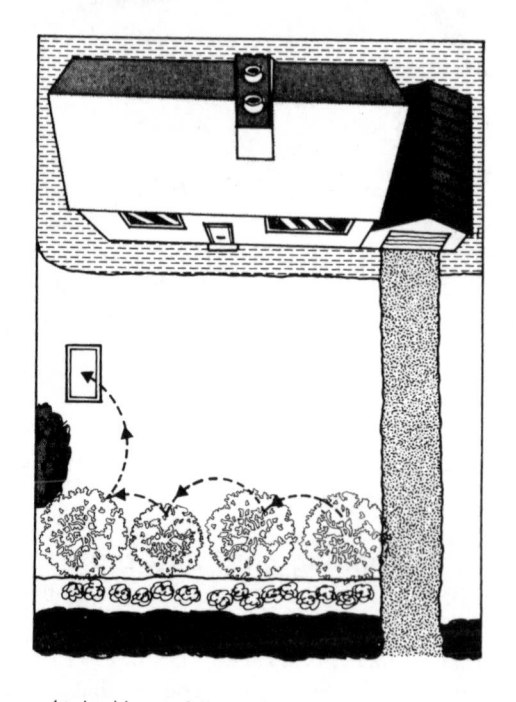

Position your bird table carefully so that it suits both the birds and you.

not feel at ease in a wide open space too far from shelter. Ideally, you should position your table so that birds can reach it by a series of short flights between bushes and trees, or a row of posts.

The distance of the bird table from the house is also important. When birds are really used to you, they will take less notice of your watching them and come to accept you as a normal part of their everyday environment, but until you have conditioned your bird visitors to this desirable degree of confidence, it is best to place the table so that any movements made by an observer just inside a window are not easily seen. Occasional visitors will also be encouraged if they are not disturbed by movements inside the house. As the use of binoculars for prolonged periods of time is tiring on eyes and wrists, the aim must eventually be to have the bird table close enough to the house to dispense with optical aids, except on special occasions when you want a particularly close view.

Hanging bird tables

Even those people who live in towns and have only a balcony or window ledge of a flat or bedsit to attract feeding birds can get a lot of enjoyment from putting up a hanging bird table.

Hanging tables can be suspended from a strong hook and wire, attached to a wall by a strong bracket, or even clamped securely to a wide window-sill. You can hang wire feeders from the table to encourage the smaller birds, or attach them close to the window of a flat or apartment, or on a balcony.

Hanging tables are ideal for those people with only a balcony
or window ledge.

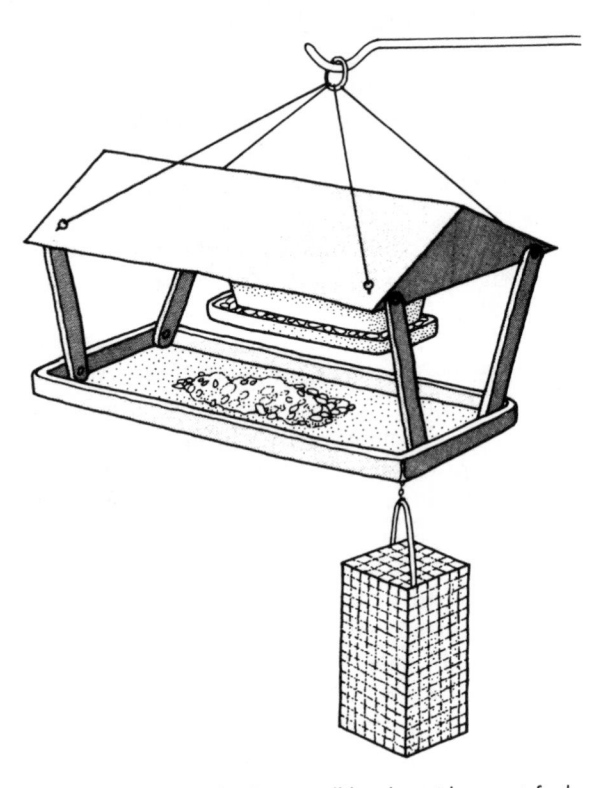

Hanging tables can be fixed to a wall bracket with peanut feeders suspended beneath.

Perching and singing posts

If you provide birds with a selection of perching posts and singing posts in the garden, you can enjoy an uninterrupted view of them from the house, as well as enjoying the delight of their songs and calls.

It is a good plan to put up a T-shaped perch made from a rustic pole about 2 metres (6 ft) high with a short transverse section on top – if possible near a drinking pool or bird bath. The birds will use it as a staging point before they go down to drink and bathe.

Male blackbirds love to sit on such a perch to sing out to all the world that the surroundings are their special territory. In fact, most bird songs – exclusive to perching birds – serve to advertise that one male has set up his territory and wants to warn off any newcomers. Each bird can have a fairly large repertoire, probably to suggest that there are plenty of birds on the patch and so further discourage new arrivals. Each species tends to sing at a particular time of year: for example, great tits and mistle thrushes tend to sing in the early spring. Some birds, like the mistle thrush, will sing regardless of the weather, but others prefer sunny days. Many birds sing at dawn and dusk, a time to listen out in particular for robins and thrushes.

Most birds have a variety of calls that they use to establish their territory, warn others of their species about danger, advertise for a mate, or give out information about food sources. The calls are designed so that they can be clearly heard

A T-shaped perch will encourage many bird visitors, especially if it is near a drinking pool or bird bath.

but are not too easy for the predator to locate, and although they are generally designed for the birds' own species, many are similar. You can buy CDs of bird songs to help you identify calls and songs but you will need to listen patiently to become expert at recognising them. The first one to learn is usually the 'teacher, teacher, teacher' call of the great tit!

If you are fortunate enough to have a pair of spotted flycatchers in your garden during the summer, you will find that another use of the perch is as a base for their acrobatic flights to capture passing insects.

Scrap baskets

Scrap baskets – which you can hang from the bird table, branches, a balcony or window-ledge – are valuable extras. I think the best models are those made of plastic-coated wire mesh with a lid. These will take mixed kitchen scraps and shelled peanuts.

Avoid scrap baskets made from collapsible wire mesh. Small birds get their feet and legs jammed between the springy wires. Never use anything that has sharp edges or points or is not strongly and safely made. Resist the temptation to buy any of the flimsy bird feeders often offered at knock-down prices in pet shops and stores. These so-called bargains can injure birds if they come apart during severe weather. Stick to products made and supplied by organisations and firms that specialise in bird furniture. You may pay a little more but it is worth the extra money to have feeders that are strong and safe, and they will also last much longer.

Seed and nut dispensers

A useful seed dispenser is one with a see-through top section so that you can check the food level, and a base that can be taken off for filling and cleaning. They should keep the seed dry in almost all weathers.

Spiral feeders for holding peanuts can be dangerous if they are too whippy; birds' legs may get trapped in the coils. Again, go for safe and well-tried models that have heavy-duty steel coils covered with PVC to prevent rusting.

There are many inexpensive devices for offering peanuts to the birds in your garden. PVC-coated metal grille baskets are excellent, and I also use the refillable nylon bags. For some inexplicable reason, siskins love to peck at peanuts suspended in red nylon mesh bags – why they go for red remains a mystery. Nowadays, many species adore peanuts and compete with the tits to swing on the baskets and bags.

If you want to put up some unshelled nuts, the best plan is to thread them on a piece of thin galvanised wire about 50 cm (20 in) long. Cut off the wire obliquely at one end to make a sharp point for skewering the nuts. Then bend the top end into a hanging hook and turn up the lower end to prevent the nuts from slipping off. When attached to the hanging point with an elastic band, the string of nuts twirls round and the birds love it – and so will you as you watch their antics.

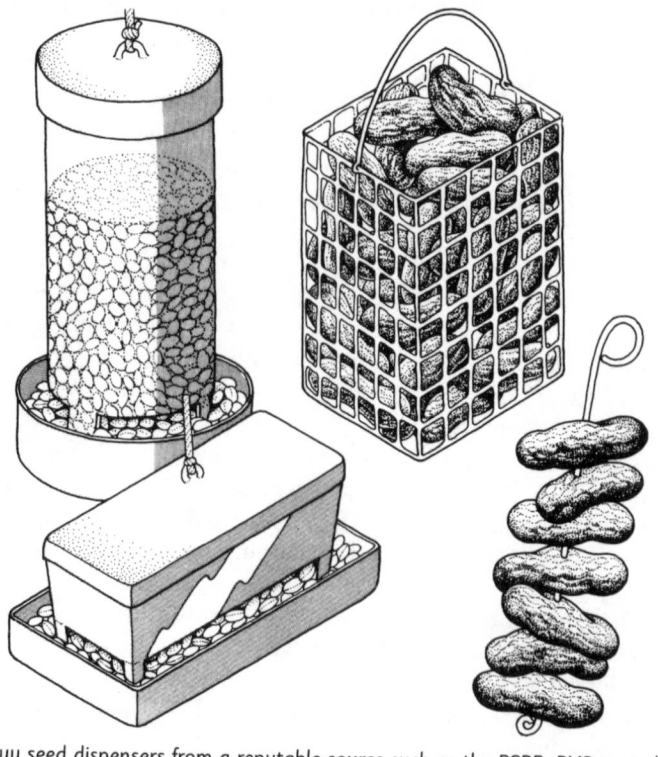

Buy seed dispensers from a reputable source such as the RSPB. PVC-coated metal grille containers are excellent peanut dispensers, or you can thread unshelled nuts onto thin galvanised wire.

Seed hoppers or peanut containers can be used in conjunction with bird tables, as they can be fixed under the roof, as well as being hung separately from trees or balconies.

Suet sticks and bells

You can buy suet sticks or make your own to hang from trees or the bird table in the garden. They are simply short, thick pieces of wood with round holes bored into the sides. I have already mentioned that you can press fat into the holes, or you can use bird pudding (see page 13) instead. Similarly, all you need to make a bird pudding or tit bell with scraps is a small cup-shaped container, which you fill with nuts and scraps and bind together with hot fat. As well as tits and nuthatches, even great spotted woodpeckers are attracted to these when they hang from the trees in your garden.

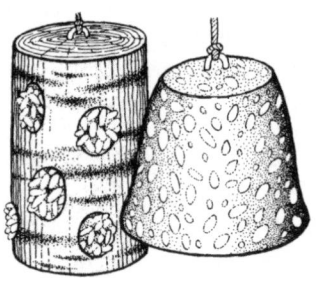

Suet sticks and tit bells are easy to make and attract tits, nuthatches and even woodpeckers.

Chapter 3

Nesting Sites and Nest Boxes

O nce you have established your feeding routine and furnished your garden with a bird table or other suitable bird furniture, you may want to think about providing plenty of natural and artificial nest sites to try to make a real success of attracting birds to your garden.

Encouraging natural nest-building

I have already mentioned providing shrubs, trees and hedges suitable for nesting, and there is much more on this in Chapter 4. Keep your hedges and shrubs well pruned, and concentrate your pruning in spring and autumn, depending on the plant, so that you can leave hedges and trees undisturbed during the breeding season.

You can help nest-building operations by leaving out in the garden some of the materials gathered by birds for nest construction. They are sharp-eyed and quickly pick up anything of use. I remember one pair of mistle thrushes that used torn-up shreds of a football match programme, and a chaffinch nest colourfully ornamented with pieces of confetti. Assemble pieces

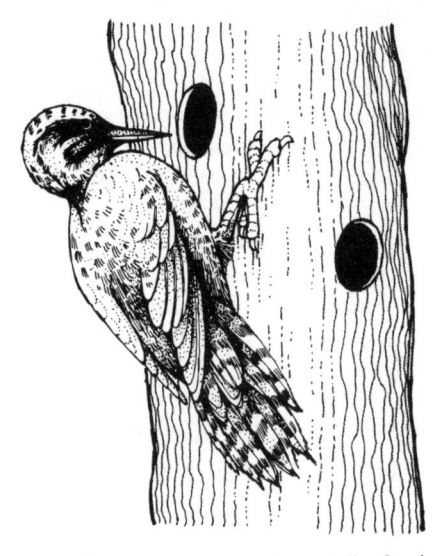

A woodpecker may be attracted to nest if you drill a few holes in an old branch or trunk.

of sheep's wool gathered from barbed wire fences on country walks; small, soft feathers or down; dried grasses and thin straw; combings of human hair or animal fur; dry leaves of oak and beech; short pieces of cotton; and rootlets dried out after digging the garden. Tuck the hair or wool into a cleft in a fence. Other material can be suspended from a tree branch in a large-mesh bag through which the birds can pull what they want. Avoid messy piles that can blow about in your own or neighbouring gardens.

Many garden birds nest in holes, and you should look round your garden and see whether there are any suitable natural holes in trees or shrubs, and whether you can make them more attractive to birds such as tits, nuthatches, tree sparrows and even woodpeckers. You may already have some old trees with holes in the decaying wood, but you can often start some of your own with the help of a brace and bit. If you drill a few holes in an old branch or trunk, a woodpecker may finish off the excavations.

Wherever possible, do not fell trees that have holes, or fill the cavities in walls and fences. If you are building a garden wall, leave some gaps suitable for pied wagtails, tits, spotted flycatchers and robins.

A lean-to or open garden shed is a wonderful haven for birds. Leave bundles of pea sticks against the side of the shed for nesting blackbirds, dunnocks and wrens. Rolls of wire netting also attract wrens and blackbirds. The shelves and ledges inside an open shed provide homes for swallows, blackbirds and robins. One year, a pair of robins nested in the sagging pocket of an old gardening coat hung up on a nail, and a friend with a dilapidated greenhouse potting shed was amused to find that robins had nested on the floor of an old bird cage without a door, which had been propped up in a corner.

Wrens will use any available nest site; an old kettle wedged in a hedge is ideal.

Robins, wrens and spotted flycatchers will build inside old kettles and cans wedged in trees, or in ivy on a wall. Make sure that the spout of the kettle points downwards so that water does not collect inside. Place all such containers well clear of the ground and shaded from direct sunshine.

Wrens will also make use of sacking to support their finely woven, domed nests. You can help them by folding a stout piece of hessian and nailing it to the underside of a bough or leaning tree trunk a few metres from the ground. You can also put sacking under the eves of a shed or garage. The idea is to create a fold or tunnel in which the wrens can build.

To encourage treecreepers, nail pieces of virgin cork or large sections of bark to a tree at such an angle that the little birds can build in the gap between the bark and the trunk.

House martins may construct their cupped mud nets under the eaves and gables of houses, but many of them are taken over by aggressive house sparrows.

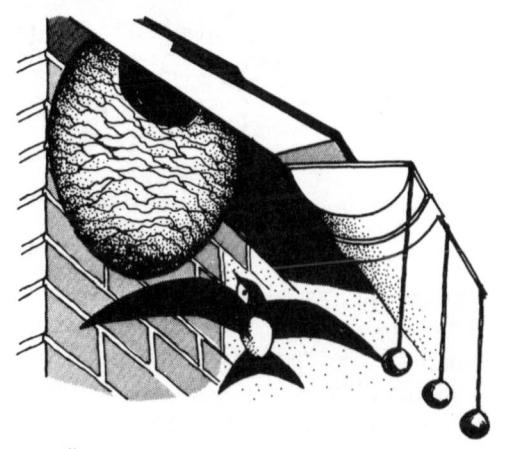

Hanging small weights on cords from the guttering will deter house sparrows from using martins' nests.

It is possible to deter sparrows from usurping martin nests by hanging a series of small weights from the guttering on pieces of string about 30 cm (12 in) long and 10 cm (4 in) apart. Martins can approach nests at a much steeper angle than the sparrows, avoiding the hanging cords.

Nest boxes

You can also buy or make your own nest boxes to place in the garden. Nest boxes are of two main designs: an enclosed box type with a small entrance hole, and trays or ledges with or without sides. Different birds prefer different types of box. Birds that nest in closed nesting boxes of various sizes include the blue tit, great tit, coal tit, marsh tit, nuthatch, redstart, house sparrow, tree sparrow, wren, treecreeper, stock dove, tawny owl, great spotted woodpecker, jackdaw, pied flycatcher and starling. Open-fronted models are preferred by robins, wrens, spotted flycatchers, pied wagtails and also jackdaws. Blackbirds and thrushes favour those with an open front and sides.

There are boxes and trays suitable for nesting owls and kestrels, but these are of interest only to those who have large gardens or areas of woodland. You can also buy wedge-shaped nest boxes especially for treecreepers. Artificial nest cups made from a plastic material are perfect for house martins. They are held in position by hooks so that you can slide them out to inspect the inside. The entrance hole for martins' nest cups should be no more than 2 cm (¾ in) deep to keep out sparrows.

Nest boxes of several types can be purchased at reasonable prices from the RSPB and from other reputable suppliers (see page 201), and the RSPB can supply you with information on making the best use of nest boxes and all kinds of bird furniture. The British Trust for Ornithology also produce a guide to nest boxes, which includes some very practical and useful information.

Making a nest box

If you are sufficiently handy, you may enjoy making your own nest boxes and other bird furniture. It is not a difficult task for the practised do-it-yourself enthusiast.

A standard nest box for smaller hole-nesting birds such as tits, wrens, redstarts, tree sparrows and nuthatches should be made from wood not less than 2 cm (¾ in) thick. Choose a hard wood if possible, as this is more durable, but cedar is the best of the soft woods and weathers well. If you can get some planks of second-hand floor boarding, this is perfect for the job.

To make the box, take a plank 1.36 m (54 in) long by 15 cm (6 in) wide and cut lengths as follows:

> 21 cm (8½ in) for the roof;
> 30 cm (12 in) for the back;
> 18 cm (7 in) for the front;
> 19 cm (7½ in) for the floor.

This will leave you with a section 48 cm (19 in) long for the sides.

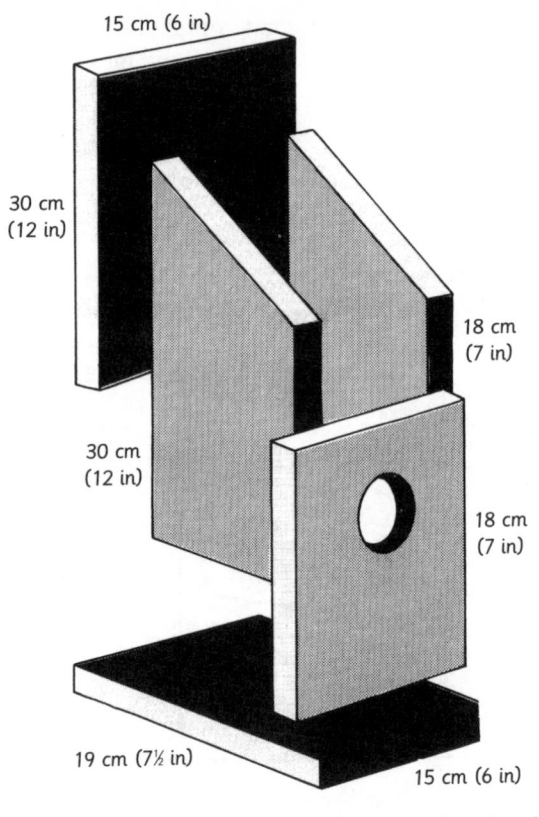

15 cm (6 in)

30 cm (12 in)

30 cm (12 in)

18 cm (7 in)

18 cm (7 in)

19 cm (7½ in)

15 cm (6 in)

A nesting box for small birds can be made using old floor boarding.

Using a pencil and ruler, mark a point 30 cm (12 in) along one edge of the remaining plank then, still measuring from the same end, mark a point 18 cm (7 in) along the other edge and join the marks with a diagonal line across the width of the plank. Cut along the line to make the sides.

Assemble the box as shown in the diagram. The sloping side pieces will support a sloping roof with a slight overhang. Fix the

A metal hole cover will prevent squirrels or woodpeckers from enlarging a nest-box hole.

joints with screws or oval nails, using a sealing compound before you nail or screw them into their final position. The nest box must be snugly fitting and completely rainproof. A wood preservative could be used, but only on the outside. You can secure the lid with screws, but most people prefer to hinge the lid with rustless metal or strips of plastic or leather so that they can lift the lid for cleaning at the end of the season.

Cut an entry hole 3 cm (1½ in) in diameter either on the side or the front of the box. The entry hole should be high up on the box, not less than 13 cm (5 in) from the floor. To prevent the hole from being enlarged by squirrels or woodpeckers, you can front the box with a piece of metal, pierced with a matching hole. (The RSPB supplies these with some of their nest boxes.) Avoid fitting a landing perch as this could assist predators. It is essential to bore a hole for drainage and ventilation in the floor of the box. Attach a wooden batten about 10 cm (4 in) wide to the back of the nest box for fixing to trees or walls.

Fixing and maintaining your nest box

Nest boxes should be fixed at a height of 2 metres (6 ft) or more from the ground on tree trunks, walls or posts in October or November. Make sure the boxes are well out of the reach of cats, rats and squirrels. They must be in positions where they neither freeze in cold winds nor grill for hours in the hot sun. The best sites face north or north-east. Open-plan nest boxes should be placed in the forks of trees and ivy-clad places where they can attract spotted flycatchers, pied wagtails and robins. Tilt them slightly so that they do not collect rain water through the entry hole. Take care when fixing the boxes to trees. If you think screws or nails may damage the tree, then fasten the box securely with leather or webbing straps.

Once the young have flown the nest, sweep out the box, then clean it with boiling water to kill any remaining parasites. Insecticides and flea powder are not recommended.

You can gain hours of enjoyment watching the birds in your garden.

A site facing north or north-east is best for a nesting box.

Chapter 4
Planning Your Miniature Bird Sanctuary

The fundamental requirements for attracting birds to your garden, whatever its size, are shelter and protection; convenient nesting sites; a constant supply of water, particularly at times of drought or hard frost; and regular supplies of food, bearing in mind the needs of particular bird species and individual tastes. Birds appreciate a change of diet as much as you do.

In the first few chapters, we looked at how you can easily supply all these needs to encourage birds into your garden. Now we are going to look in more detail at how the keen birdwatcher can do even more, turning the garden into a miniature sanctuary, planned and planted with the needs of the birds in mind – and, incidentally, giving a colourful and attractive result that any landscape artist would be proud of! The aim is to attract a greater number and variety of birds to your garden and home area, and any initial outlay on equipment or suitable trees, shrubs and plants will quickly bring its own rewards and pleasures. In any event, you can plan any changes to your garden to be made over a number of seasons, minimising upheaval and cost.

I am often asked to define the best kind of bird garden and miniature sanctuary. The truth is that the ideal bird sanctuary would hardly be a garden, in the true sense of the word, but rather a mixture of trees, shrubs and flowers with a good supply of weeds and tangled, jungle corners. There would be nettle beds, brambles, old tree stumps and old tin cans and kettles on the ground and in forks of trees in which robins and wrens could build their nests.

Naturally, this sort of layout does not appeal to the tidy person who wants a neat, well-ordered flower, shrub and vegetable garden. If you are to have the best of both worlds you must aim for a compromise, particularly if your garden is a small one, but that is not difficult to do, and you can make your own choices on how cultivated or how wild your own garden should be.

Planning your mini-sanctuary

While many gardeners will be modifying an established layout, some will be starting from scratch. Naturally, it is impossible to suggest a scheme to fit all requirements. Gardens come in so many different shapes and sizes, with so many types of soil, that I can only give a set of guidelines and leave the individual to work out the best plan according to local conditions and the available budget.

The best way to go about it is to draw some rough plans of your existing garden, marking in all the features that are to remain: large trees and shrubs, for example, or existing features that you wish to keep. You can then sketch in new features for your ideal bird sanctuary, with details of the arrangement of any new beds or rockeries, and some suggested planting schemes. You need to look at a list of priorities and start thinking about the practicalities of where to start, which will inevitably include many changes of the mind along the way, but that should all be part of the enjoyment. In this chapter, we'll look at some of the important features that will help to make your mini-sanctuary attractive to birds. As we have said, there must be a compromise between the practical needs of the gardener and the requirements of a small sanctuary. Your main aim is to provide the basic essentials.

The first things to think about is shelter. On one side of your bird garden you will therefore need a hedge to provide cover and nest sites, and on another a row or groups of fast-growing, leafy shrubs with plenty of branching wood for perches and nests. You will then make sure that young birds in the nests have concealment from enemies and shelter from hot sun and rain. If

You can grow all kinds of plants to encourage birds in your garden.

you study the direction of the prevailing wind in your area, you will be able to work out the best planting programme to give birds cover. In Britain, the prevailing winds are generally from the west, but as my garden is in a high position exposed to the usually colder northerly and easterly winds, I have made sure that my evergreen hedges cut off the worst of the gusts from those directions.

The other essentials are a variety of levels, provided by rockeries or low stone walls; a lawn easily viewed from one of the main windows; and a wild patch where brambles, nettles and other plants normally classed as weeds can be allowed to grow. Your selection of suitable plants can be encouraged with a rustic archway, pergola or arbour for climbers such as honeysuckle and roses, which produce edible berries, and trellises for training berry-bearing evergreens. You'll also need a supply of water from a bird bath or small pond, and many birds love to take advantage of perches and posts (see page 32).

Though the key to all your planning is the welfare of the birds, careful selection and positioning of your plants will accentuate the beauty of flowers and foliage, so that your garden is a charming setting for your home life as well as for the birds. Whatever you plant, consider the effect from the main windows of the house – your principal observation point. There will be some secluded areas that are not visible from the house, of course, but you can usually place trees and shrubs so that they can be seen from one or more windows.

Although I have listed details of some of the best trees, shrubs and plants you can consider for your garden, avid gardeners will find plenty more in the pages of their gardening books or by investigating their local garden centres. Since most plants can be bought in containers, you can start your collection at almost any season apart from the depths of winter, then plant them out at a suitable time when the weather becomes warmer.

Hedges

One of the reasons why Britain has such a large population of song birds compared with other countries is its profusion of hedges, spinneys and small tracts of open, mixed woodland. Since many farmland hedges are being bulldozed to make fields bigger and to make it easier to use the large machines that are part and parcel of modern agricultural practice, it makes it even more vital to try to redress the balance by creating your own hedges and banks in the garden, as well as protecting any farm hedges where you can.

Hedges are a vital part of attracting a varied bird population into your garden. They provide protection from the wind, valuable sources of food, and ideal nesting places for smaller birds. In my own garden I have a sweetbriar rose hedge that offers dense, prickly cover for nesting birds. In winter, greenfinches come to eat the profusion of scarlet hips. The fragrance of the foliage after a summer shower perfumes the whole garden – it always reminds me of the scent of ripe apples.

Like us, birds hate to be buffeted and frozen by icy blasts of wind, especially in spring when the nesting season is in full swing, and hedges offer the perfect solution. To cut off the winds on the north side of my garden, I have a tall hedge of *Cotoneaster lacteus*. This attractive evergreen, with its arching branches and tall growth, bears creamy-white flowers in summer and is decked with dark red berries in winter. Flocks of fieldfares and redwings, which come to Britain from Scandinavia for the cold months of the year, join the garden blackbirds and thrushes to make short work of the berries as soon as there is a nip in the air. Smaller birds hunt for insects at the base of the hedge and the screen of tough, dark green leaves gives welcome protection from the worst of the wind, rain, sleet and snow. Another good subject for hedging is *Cotoneaster simondsii*.

Thorny hedges and trees are very much favoured by birds because of the protection they afford against all kinds of nest

Cotoneaster varieties make good hedging plants and shrubs.

55

robber – human and animal. In my first garden I planted a hawthorn hedge that grew quickly and provided nest sites for blackbirds, song thrushes, whitethroats, wrens, dunnocks, greenfinches and linnets. A boundary hedge of this type also offers winter shelter and food. Thrushes, blackbirds, redwings and fieldfares eat the hawthorn berries, and small birds like tits, wrens and dunnocks forage among the leaves and natural litter along the hedge bottom for insects, larvae, woodlice and centipedes. Hawthorn can be clipped to form quite a thick hedge, proof against dogs or vandals and providing valuable nest cover. Individual trees or hedges are good for berries and the varieties with red or pink flowers add rich colour to the garden scene. They are often grown with blackthorn.

In one corner of the garden I have planted a clump of laurel, which is kept well trimmed to ensure bushy growth and act as a protective hedge in that area of the garden. It offers dense cover and is tenanted in spring and summer by nesting blackbirds and thrushes. But a word of advice: do not overdo the planting of

Hawthorn makes an excellent hedging plant.

laurel, or of rhododendrons or azaleas. Shrubs of this kind block light from the ground, fail to attract insects, and do not provide good sites for nesting. Personally, I am not very fond of privet as a hedging subject either, although it does offer cover and purple berries that attract bullfinches.

Trees

Trees and shrubs are important in a bird garden. They provide protection, nesting and roosting places and, of course, food, so those that produce a plentiful crop of berries are especially welcomed by the bird gardener. The most important thing when planting trees is to consider their size. Most of us have relatively small gardens, so stick to small trees that will not outgrow their usefulness.

In planting new trees, select native rather than foreign species and, as I cannot stress too much, make sure you know the final size and growth pattern of the tree. Few small gardens can support forest trees like the oak, even if you have the time to wait for such slow-growing trees to mature. If you have the space, such a tree will develop and attract and support its own large community of birds and the insects on which they feed, but it is not appropriate in most gardens. Similarly, you are probably best to avoid trees with a very fast rate of growth, such as poplars and willows. These trees may look beautiful but they grow phenomenally quickly and can undermine foundations if planted too close to a building, as well as blocking out much of the light. Opt instead for faster-growing but smaller trees such as ash or silver birch. In my own garden I have a splendid silver birch that is a feature of the front lawn and attracts many birds. Siskins come to feed on its seeds in winter, and many other species use its spreading branches for perching and hunting for insects throughout the year.

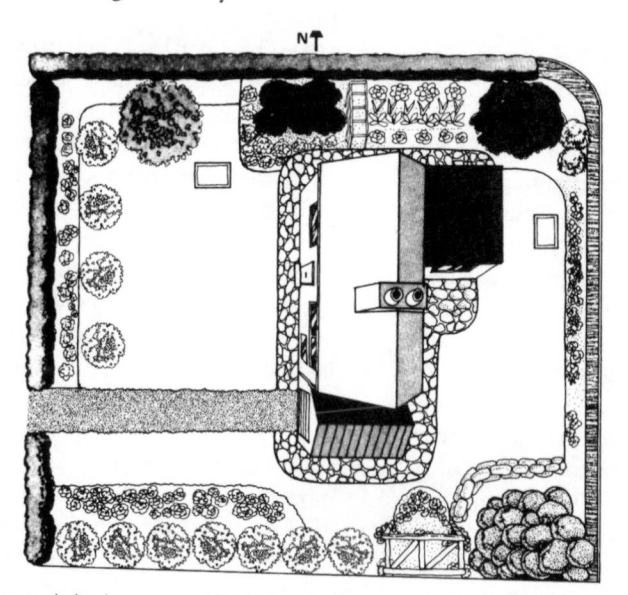

Trees and shrubs can provide shelter and nesting places, as well as berries, to attract birds.

If you have room in the garden, fruit trees are good for birds, as well as providing you with fresh fruit in season. Old apple and pear trees attract a great many birds, particularly tits, finches, robins and nuthatches. Greenfinches, chaffinches and goldfinches often like to nest in them. A friend who left an old, gnarled apple tree at the bottom of his garden was rewarded with a nesting pair of nuthatches who commandeered a hole in the lichen-covered trunk. Leave some fruit on the trees in autumn and you will be certain to attract blackbirds, song and mistle thrushes, redwings and fieldfares. Varieties suitable for fan-training may be more suitable for smaller gardens.

Go easy on the larger conifers. They can grow very tall, and their dense masses of needles keep out light and suppress plant growth on the ground underneath their branches. They also require a lot of water and dry out the ground beneath, taking a lot of goodness with the water. I have only a few of the more compact fastigiate (upright) varieties. These include the golden form of the yew, a couple of Irish junipers and a *Cupressus*

Yew is a slow-growing plant suitable for larger gardens.

arizonica conica, which has pretty, bluish-green foliage. Linnets and dunnocks (hedge sparrows) regularly nest in them. The yew is a valuable evergreen that makes a good hedge and offers nest sites, although it grows slowly and may take many years to produce the berries which are a favourite food of thrushes, blackbirds and starlings. The birds eat the pulp but pass out the poisonous seeds harmlessly. Yew bark and needles are poisonous.

Rowan trees, or mountain ash, are recommended for their big crops of glistening red and orange berries in August, greatly loved by thrushes and bullfinches. There are also varieties with pink or yellow berries. They make a graceful feature in the corner of a garden, with brilliant russet leaf colours in autumn.

Some gardeners think of the common elder as a pest, but the bird gardener who has a wild corner could grow one or two

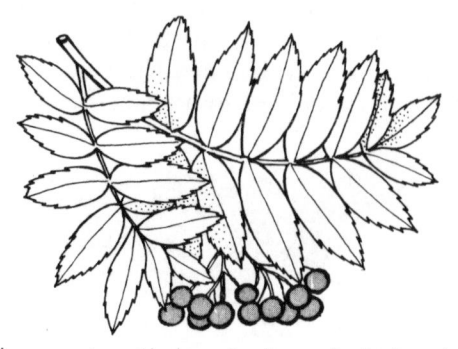

The rowan is an ideal tree for the smaller bird garden.

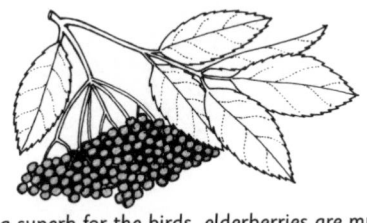

As well as being superb for the birds, elderberries are much in demand among makers of home-made wine!

bushes for the vivid purple berries, which are eaten greedily by many species of bird, especially the thrush and tit families. Migrant warblers love to dally among the elder fruits on mellow autumn days. The tree has a lank, open growth and needs pruning to give the best effect, but the fragrant white flowers provide a lovely display in season.

Shrubs

Both as a tree and as a shrub, the evergreen holly is excellent in every way. Well-grown trees or bushes give shelter and roosting places, while the berries are eaten by the thrush tribe. As they are fairly slow growing, they are not likely to overrun a small garden. But don't forget that hollies are either male or female; only the female tree produces the berries, and you must have a male nearby for cross-fertilisation. Hollies also make excellent hedging plants. Near my home, an enterprising water company has planted a long holly hedge, always kept neatly trimmed,

Hollies make an excellent choice for a hedge or shrub.

round its pumping station and the houses of employees. This smart hedge is a paradise for nesting birds as well as being a much-admired feature of the landscape.

The cultivated forms of barberry, *berberis,* are useful in the bird garden because their bright red and orange berries contain vitamin C and they provide good nest sites for blackbirds, thrushes and finches. They make good hedges, with the added bonus of yellow and orange flowers in season and some beautiful red or gold foliage, and they can be grown in all types

Berberis varieties combine beautiful foliage with bird-friendly berries.

of soil. There are plenty of varieties to choose from, both deciduous and evergreen. *Berberis stenophylla* and *Berberis darwinii* are particularly good, as long as they are kept trimmed, otherwise they can become lanky. *Berberis vulgaris, Berberis thunbergii* and *Berberis aggregata* are also good choices.

I have mentioned *Cotoneaster lacteus* as an excellent evergreen hedging plant, but it can also be trained against a wall or fence, as can *Cotoneaster buxifolia* and *Cotoneaster francheti.* There are also many other useful members of the Cotoneaster family that are ideal for the bird garden both for berries and leafy cover. *Cotoneaster horizontalis,* sometimes known as the fishbone cotoneaster, and *Cotoneaster rotundifolia* grow to more than a metre high and can also be trained against a wall. Their berries attract flocks of waxwings when these handsome Scandinavian birds come to Britain in winter. *Cotoneaster dammeri* and *Cotoneaster prostrata* have a trailing habit.

Viburnums can be planted for their berries and the vivid colour of their autumn leaves, but remember that the berries are poisonous to mammals. Two native varieties of viburnum are *Viburnum lantana* (sometimes known as the wayfaring tree) and *Viburnum opulus* (the guelder rose), the latter a truly wild plant that has a crop of shiny glutinous berries much loved by birds but that does demand quite a lot of space. The cultivated variety *Viburnum compactum* is preferable if space is at a premium.

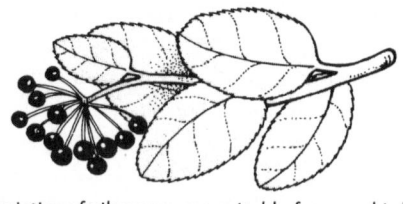

Several varieties of viburnum are suitable for your bird garden.

Euonymus europaeus, sometimes called spindle, is also worth growing for its pink and orange fruits. Birds love the berries, and feed off the quantities of insects the plant supports although, like viburnum, the berries are poisonous to mammals. Euonymus prefers a chalky soil.

The yellow-berried *Pyracantha rogersiana* against my front wall gets stripped of its fruit by thrushes and blackbirds, but only after they have first raided the red-berried pyracanthas. The same is true of the yellow-berried rowan called Joseph Rock.

Euonymus is an excellent shrub to grow for its berries.

Cultivated blackberries supply fruit for both you and the birds.

I find that my Oregon thornless blackberry, trained against a fence, attracts warblers and finches in late summer when there is a huge crop of berries. Sometimes little family parties of bullfinches, piping plaintively to each other, come to peck at the ripe fruit. I pick plenty of blackberries, then leave a few for the birds; in any event, they always seem to be able to reach the fruit I miss.

Other suitable shrubs include escallonias, ceanothus, rambler roses, clematis, wisteria. The wisteria is a particular favourite nesting place of the spotted flycatcher.

When choosing shrubs and trees, pay attention to the ultimate texture provided by the twigs, branches and leaves. Birds need to be able to move about freely inside bush cover, and a hen bird sitting on her nest must be able to slip away quickly if danger threatens, unhampered by too much thick growth.

To make your garden a true sanctuary where a number of bird species will nest and migrants can find cover and food, you must ensure that trees and shrubs are not allowed to get too lanky. As a general rule most bushes and shrubs are best for birds when they are trimmed and pruned to give bushy growth. Aim to keep trees at a medium height, taking into account their natural growth patterns and rate of growth. Prune hedges and shrubs to form the maximum number of fork structures strong enough to support nests. Cut the branches so that each fork contains at least three branches. The fork should be at an angle of 70 degrees, facing vertically upwards. At the other extreme, some gardeners make a fetish of closely clipped low hedges. These may look wonderfully neat, but they leave no room for birds to manoeuvre and are usually shunned.

Roosting places

Hedges, trees and shrubs are also great roosting places for birds. During the winter, birds must spend 16 hours a day at roost. They can lose a lot of body heat and therefore like to choose a place out of the wind and rain. They need the cover of evergreens or thickets and you must always think of this aspect when laying out the bird garden. It is best to have a variety of compact evergreens grown in clumps. Thick ivy, grown on a south-facing wall or fence, is much used by roosting birds. Close-foliaged conifers, such as some of the upright cypresses, are often chosen by dunnocks, robins, finches and sparrows for roosting. Fir trees, with a more open growing habit, do not offer such a dense cover or such good protection from wind and weather.

Keep bushes and shrubs pruned for bushy growth to
encourage nesting birds.

Building on different levels

Any bird garden should be built with a variety of levels that give birds shelter and provide areas where they can safely feed. When I made my present garden around a new house, one of my first jobs was to build a low stone wall that could be viewed

Different levels in the garden provide shelter and feeding places.

from one of the large picture windows. The raised bed, covered with low-growing shrubs and plants, is a happy hunting ground for birds at all seasons of the year and does not get snowed up in winter. Song thrushes and blackbirds love to prod for food among the plants that trail over the wall. The thrushes find snails under the leaves and use some of the flat stones as anvils to break them open.

Hollows and rockeries

Other important places where birds look for food are little hollows, banks and sheltered nooks where they can forage contentedly for insects and seeds out of the worst of wind and weather, and under the protection of leaves and low branches. When you are planning your garden, you should therefore try to introduce various levels so that you can create such bird-friendly areas.

South-facing rockeries with an irregular jumble of stones and plants are popular with the smaller birds. There they can find many small insects, slugs, snails and woodlice among the crevices and rocks or under leaves. During dry spells, you will find a rockery frequently visited by thrushes, blackbirds and dunnocks. Here they will find slugs, caterpillars and insects among the cool, moist leaves of alpine plants and succulents that have not been shrivelled up by the glaring sun like some of the other plants in the garden.

A well-kept lawn

One of the major sources of food for common garden birds is the animal life that lives in the lawn, so a well-kept lawn or area of turf is a fundamental requisite of a bird garden. There you can easily see birds through your windows as they hunt for worms, beetle grubs and ants. I never tire of watching blackbirds, thrushes and robins as they listen and look with heads turned to one side, then pounce on their hidden prey and pull it out of the grass. It is a remarkable example of co-ordination of acute eyesight and hearing. Not only do the worms in your lawn and garden do a most valuable job in the garden by aerating, draining and enriching the soil, they are also an important part of the daily diet of birds.

Wild area

If you have room at the end of the garden for a patch of rough grass, brambles and nettles, or a wild area under trees, then include it in your plan. A nettle bed not only provides an area where small birds can search for insects, and low cover where some species can build nests, it is also the feeding place for the caterpillars of the peacock, small tortoise-shell and red admiral butterflies. You do need to keep an eye on your wild area, though, to make sure the nettles and other plants do not get out of hand and invade the rest of the garden where you do not want them. If you have wild blackberry briars, make sure you trim them back as they will root from the ends of long stems.

Flowers and smaller plants

We have already mentioned how much birds enjoy a rockery, and there you can plant the small alpines and succulents that provide shelter for insects on which the birds can feed, especially during dry weather.

I have plenty of honeysuckle growing along my fences, but they can also be trained over a pergola or rustic archway, or over an old tree stump or post. There are both evergreen and deciduous varieties, and you can choose from different colours of foliage and flower, from yellow to dark red. Some varieties also have a wonderful fragrance. They bunch up to give thick cover for nests, and their luscious berries are eaten by blackbirds, tits, bullfinches and warblers.

Another bush I keep for its berries as well as its flowers is the so-called Himalayan honeysuckle (*Leycesteria formosa*). Birds adore the fleshy purple berries.

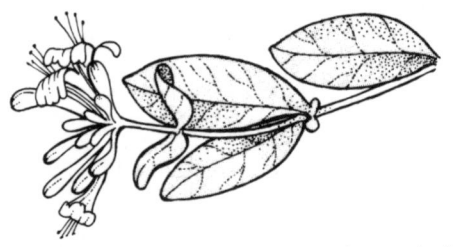

Choose a scented honeysuckle so you can enjoy the wonderful fragrance on summer evenings.

71

Ivy is also useful for attracting birds to walls and fences, or for growing over unsightly tree stumps. Although it has a bad reputation for growing too quickly and strangling plants, not all varieties are rampant, and it does provide valuable cover and berries in the bird garden. The varieties with variegated leaves are particularly attractive. The thrush family eat the dark berries, while wrens and other small birds like the cover of the evergreen leaves. Old ivy clumps are favourite nest sites for pied wagtails and spotted flycatchers.

Some annual and perennial plants grown in the flower garden bear seeds that birds like to eat. I grew up on an Essex nursery where many flower-seed crops were grown and I remember with pleasure the tinkling flocks of goldfinches that used to raid the seeding heads of French and African marigolds, godetia (clarkia) and cornflower. All these flowers are easy to grow in the garden. If you leave the seed heads on the plants as long as possible, you are likely to attract many finches to the garden.

There are many attractive varieties of ivy.

It is a good plan to grow some sunflowers. Not only are these stately plants so attractive in the garden, but greenfinches find their seeds irresistible. Finches also like the seeds of gaillardia, cosmos, linum (flax), sweet sultan and summer chrysanthemums. I have also noticed that bullfinches are fond of the seeds of delphinium, antirrhinum, larkspur and pansies.

Water

An adequate supply of water is one of the most important points to bear in mind when you are establishing your garden bird sanctuary. No garden that lacks this facility will attract bird life; drinking water is essential, and places for bathing and preening are equally important. We have already looked at the importance of providing water in Chapter 1 (see page 19), but if you wish, you could create your own garden pond for your miniature sanctuary.

Garden centres stock many sizes and shapes of ready-made pond liners, which need to be laid on to soft sand so that they bed down well and the liner does not come into contact with any sharp stones that could pierce the base. Alternatively, you could line a pond with concrete, then seal it with bituminous paint or a heavy-gauge polythene liner. A pond should hold no less than 60 litres (13 gallons) and should have both deeper and shallow water, especially if you want to encourage birds to bathe there. Small birds like a depth of about 3 cm (1¼ in), so make sure there is a gentle slope on at least one side. Most

Oxygenating aquatic plants in your pond will help to keep the water clear.

ready-made ponds are constructed with a shallow shelf. Do not site the pond too close to any shrubbery, which may conceal a cat or other predator. You can buy pumps and fountains to help circulate the water in the pond and keep it fresh; your garden centre will specify the size of pump for the quantity of water in the pond. You should also stock the pond with some oxygenating plants. These plants will grow in a few centimetres of soil covered by shallow water: *Sagittaria graminea*, *Isoetes lacustris* (quillwort), *Tillaea recurva*, *Eleocharis acicularis*, *Hottonia palustris* (water violet) and *Callitriche autumnalis*. Birds are attracted to the insects that come to the water plants as well as to the water itself for drinking, bathing and preening.

Combating problems

When you are considering the profit-and-loss account of birds in your garden sanctuary, remember that even common and obtrusive birds like the house sparrows and starlings eat their share of insects, which are garden pests. On balance, the presence of birds is beneficial to a well-organised garden and there is the welcome bonus of their colour and vivacity to enhance the beauty of your trees, shrubs, flowers and lawns.

However, you should remember that a garden that attracts a wide range of bird life also has its own special problems. You may need to take precautions against attacks by birds on fruit, seedlings, salad and green crops. Blackbirds find strawberries and other soft fruit irresistible and they will take their share of your cherries. House sparrows, wood pigeons and other birds can play havoc with tender greenery. Sparrows are particularly troublesome in spring when they peck at crocuses and polyanthus blooms. However, the money you will need to spend on netting and black cotton to keep the birds off your most valued crops and flower beds is a small price to pay for the many hours of pleasure you get from watching and listening to the garden birds.

Bullfinches are among the most colourful birds in the garden but they are as much a problem to the gardener as they are to the professional fruit grower. In winter and early spring they eat the buds of many fruit trees, lilac and forsythia. The worst bullfinch raids on fruit buds follow those autumns when their natural foods are in short supply. For most people, the number of such birds in the garden will be relatively small, so they should not pose a problem. However, if you are fortunate enough to attract bullfinches in number, you may want to take some action to protect your trees and shrubs. You cannot always be on the alert to scare away marauding bullfinches, so the most effective remedy I can recommend is a cobwebby material available from garden centres, which can be draped over the branches. This substance makes the fruit trees look unsightly during the vulnerable period but it certainly works as an effective deterrent.

Jays and magpies are other unwelcome callers, and certainly magpies are becoming more common garden visitors. They steal fruit and green peas and raid nests, eating both eggs and young birds. I am afraid there is little you can do to prevent these bold and greedy members of the crow family from raiding the garden. I suppose it is some compensation that both species have such handsome plumage. I particularly admire the bright blue and black wing flashes of the jay. When I was a boy growing up in an Essex village, the best Sunday hats of my father and all his farming friends were adorned with bunches of these bright feathers – evidence that many jays had paid the ultimate price of their sorties into the rows of green peas in local gardens and allotments.

Boundaries

While hedges are a vital part of a bird garden, they can generate disputes and disagreements between neighbours so, before we move on, let us look at the law and how it relates to hedges, so that you can avoid any problems.

Arguments are chiefly about size, height and tidiness, and about cutting the hedge, particularly in the breeding season. It is an offence under Section 1 of the Wildlife and Countryside Act of 1981 intentionally to take, damage or destroy the nest of any wild bird while it is in use or being built. It will be an intentional act, for example, if you or your neighbour know there is an active nest in the hedge, yet still cut the hedge, damaging or destroying the nest in the process.

A boundary hedge is normally the joint responsibility of both neighbours. Both must agree on major work, including removal, coppicing or layering. In theory, you need your neighbour's agreement before you even start trimming the hedge. If the hedge is just inside your neighbour's garden, he or she owns it; you have the right only to trim parts that encroach the boundary line.

Your neighbour should ask for your permission for access to trim the hedge on your property. Regardless of ownership, no one can trim or cut a hedge if the action damages active birds' nests and, hence, violates the Wildlife and Countryside Act.

If tall hedges or trees put your garden in the shade, you can cut off branches that overhang your boundary. You can also prune back roots that invade your property, even if this is detrimental to the plant. You do not have the right to cut down vegetation on your neighbour's property, or apply weedkiller to destroy the plants. (Birds and the law, see page 194.)

Chapter 5
Birds to Encourage in Your Garden

n this chapter, I have selected and briefly described the birds that you are most likely to see in your garden. Some are year-round residents; others are migrants and stay only for a short period in the summer or winter; others may live in surrounding habitats, such as woodland, but visit the garden occasionally. Some are confident and outgoing birds that you will see regularly – such as the cheeky robin – while others are shy and may only occasionally venture near the house but there is a good chance you will see them if you watch regularly and carefully. Obviously putting out food on a regular basis and erecting nest boxes will encourage more species to visit your garden.

The birds are organised in families of birds, starting with the most common and the smaller species. The illustrations of the birds should help you to identify the visitors to your garden. For each bird, I have given its Latin name and approximate size. Next to that are a pair of silhouettes: one of the bird in question and one of a sparrow which will give you a comparison of size and shape. Where the sparrow is perching on a branch, the sparrow silhouette is on the right-hand side. Where the birds are standing on the ground, the sparrow is on the left.

Blue tits are among the most popular visitors to bird gardens.
Hang half-coconuts to encourage them, either upside-down or
with a drainage hole drilled through the coconut.

Robin

Erithacus rubecula

Length 14 cm (5½ in)

Britain's most popular garden bird because of its jaunty habits and tameness, the robin can be seen in gardens throughout the year. It often follows the gardener to get worms and grubs turned up by the spade and you can even attract some robins to eat from your hand if you offer a regular supply of mealworms, which they find irresistible (see page 14). In winter, robins are regular and quite aggressive visitors to the bird table, often chasing off other birds of much greater size and weight. Favourite foods are nuts, seeds, oats, bird pudding, biscuit and bread crumbs, and kitchen scraps. The male and female both have the familiar red-breasted plumage, but the young are mottled brown. Robins naturally nest in holes in trees and walls or in thick ivy, but can be attracted to build if you put out old kettles and tray-type, open-fronted wooden nest boxes.

Blackbird

Turdus merula

Length 25 cm (10 in)

A very common bird that can be seen in the garden all the year round, especially in suburban areas, the striking glossy-black plumage and yellow eye ring are confined to the cock blackbird; hens are brown with a slightly mottled breast, while the young are reddish-brown and speckled. Blackbirds feed both in the open and in undergrowth but rarely stray too far from the cover of bushes and shrubs. They love gardens with lawns where they can search for earthworms, and can often be seen with their heads cocked on one side, sensing the activity beneath the soil. Blackbirds are frequent visitors to the bird table and ground feeding stations, where they like to eat fat, seeds, bird pudding, apples, cheese, sultanas and kitchen scraps. The blackbird's beautiful fluted song and rattling 'mik-mik-mik' alarm call are the most familiar sounds of the bird garden. Blackbirds nest in hedges, evergreen bushes, ivy clumps and ledges of outhouses but will also use a nest tray or an open-fronted nest box.

Starling

Sturnus vulgaris

Length 21.5 cm (8½ in)

One of the most common garden birds, the starling has a long, yellow, pointed bill and a wonderful purple-green sheen to its dark plumage in the breeding season. In winter, the plumage is more heavily marked with white, and the bill is darker. The juvenile is more grey. The starling has a short tail and pointed, triangular wings. A sociable bird, starlings can often been seen in large flocks, and some of these flocks may be immigrants from the Continent. An aggressive feeder, starlings will push other birds away from the bird table or ground feeding stations, but cannot compete as well on hanging containers, and are always wary of human movement in the garden or at the windows of the house. They nest in holes of trees and walls, and in drainpipes. If the wood of a nest box is soft, they will enlarge the entry holes of smaller birds such as tits. Starlings eat almost any food that is offered in the garden, being particularly fond of household scraps, but they also help the gardener by eating many grubs and pests, as well as seeds and soft fruits.

Song Thrush

Turdus philomelos

Length 23 cm (9 in)

A friend of the gardener, destroying many pests, the song thrush loves to eat snails, smashing open the shells on stones or paving slabs. It likes to feed on the ground but is rather nervous and wary. It eats household scraps, fruit and cheese, and is particularly fond of sultanas. Like the other thrushes, it loves old apples and berries. Slightly smaller than the mistle thrush, the song thrush is brown on top, mottled brown and white underneath, with large, dark eyes. It nests in bushes, ivy clumps and sometimes on the ledges of buildings. One of the finest of our garden songsters, the thrush's song has repeated musical phrases, which prevents confusion with the mistle thrush or blackbird. Numbers have declined in recent years, although they can still be seen in gardens throughout the year.

Mistle Thrush

Turdus viscivorus

Length 27 cm (10½ in)

The largest British thrush, this bird takes its name from its fondness for mistletoe berries, as it is primarily a bird of the open woodland. It is more upright than the song thrush, with a longer tail and wings. Its feathers are grey-brown on top with a pale front dotted with large spots, and white tips to the outer tail feathers. The young are mottled brown with a pale neck. The mistle thrush has a distinctive dipping flight during which it makes a churring call. The mistle thrush can be attracted to bird tables in hard weather by a supply of sultanas and bird pudding. You should also put out old apples on the ground as it finds these irresistible. Sometimes known as the storm cock, mistle thrushes are very fond of berries, particularly cotoneaster and hawthorn. If you have tall, old trees with ivy clumps you may encourage mistle thrushes to nest in a fork, or along a branch, in early spring.

Fieldfare

Turdus pilaris

Length 25 cm (10 in)

A winter visitor to British gardens from Scandinavia, the fieldfare is mainly to be seen in Scottish or northern gardens. It flies like a mistle thrush but has a chuckling 'chack-chack' call. Distinguished by its pale grey head and rump, chestnut back and almost black tail, it comes into the garden to eat berries on shrubs and trees and also likes old apples put down on the ground in frosty and snowy weather. It comes to bird tables for scraps, fruit and berries, and will turn over stones on the ground to seek out invertebrates. If possible, leave some apples on your trees in autumn to encourage flocks of fieldfares into the garden from the open fields.

Redwing

Turdus iliacus

Length 21 cm (8¼ in)

Like the fieldfare, this is a winter visitor from Norway and Sweden and mainly comes to northern areas of Britain. It is a small and delicate thrush, which cannot endure long cold spells. It comes into the garden to feed on berries and snails, and large flocks can be seen in grassy fields as they search for worms. It will come to ground feeding stations for berries, seeds, scraps and old apples, and is particularly fond of hawthorn berries. Look for its distinctive chestnut-red blank patches and bold white eye stripe, as well as its streaked rather than spotted brown and white breast. Its song is a distinctive series of four to seven descending notes, which can be heard from quite a long distance.

House Sparrow

Passer domesticus

Length 14.5 cm (5¾ in)

This common and gregarious British bird, which benefits so much from living in close proximity to people, is less numerous in Britain than it used to be. Intelligent and resourceful, the sparrow was once regarded as a pest in some areas because it tended to crowd out less robust species by its sheer energy and force of numbers. It tends to be chirpy and adaptable, although it can be fairly aggressive and numerous at bird tables and ground feeding stations. Sparrows will enjoy all kinds of foods on the bird table, but especially go for insects and weed seeds. Keen gardeners may find it hard to forgive the fact that sparrows attack their crocuses and other spring flowers. The female is a mottled brown, while the male can be differentiated by his grey cap and black bib and the stronger pattern on his grey and brown plumage. House sparrows nest in trees and hedges, and are also aggressive usurpers of nest boxes and house martins' nests.

Tree Sparrow

Passer montanus

Length 14 cm (5½ in)

Smaller and slimmer than the house sparrow, the tree sparrow is more at home in farm or heathland, but does visit gardens for household scraps and seeds, although it is a shyer bird and not usually a match for the more overbearing house sparrow. It will join a mixed flock of finches and buntings to feed on corn, seeds and scraps put down on the ground in the garden. Look for the chocolate-brown head and neck (the top of the house sparrow's head is grey), black spots on a white cheek, pale brown breast and brown and black upper parts, black chin and double white wing bars. For nesting, they like old trees with holes in the trunks, ivy clumps and thatched roofs, and you can attract tree sparrows to the garden by putting up enclosed nest boxes with 2.75 cm (1⅛ in) diameter entry holes. Its voice is more musical and metallic than that of the house sparrow.

Dunnock

Prunella modularis

Length 14.5 cm (5¾ in)

A common and unobtrusive garden bird, the dunnock, also known as the hedge sparrow, has a grey head and breast with streaked brown upper parts. Its bill is longer and thinner than that of the house sparrow, and its shape is plumper and more like a robin. It spends much of its time on the ground or in low vegetation, moving forward with short jerks or a curious shuffling walk, frequently flicking its wings. In autumn and winter it comes to ground feeding stations for crumbs, cake and seeds, but is not a frequent visitor to bird tables. Its main food is insects, but it will also eat seeds of all kinds, especially in winter. The dunnock has a lively, warbling song delivered in jerky bursts. It nests in hedges and evergreen bushes but you can often encourage it to nest by leaving a bunch of pea sticks against a fence or wall.

Wren

Troglodytes troglodytes
Length 9.5 cm (3¾ in)

The smallest brown bird in the garden, the wren has long been a favourite. A tiny bird with beautiful brown barred feathers and a distinctive cocked tail, it is most often seen on the ground, creeping about in search of insects and spiders with its long, thin bill. Its wings beat rapidly when it makes its characteristic short, direct flights from perch to perch. It likes the cover of shrubberies and ivy-covered walls and so is not a frequent visitor to feeding stations, but you can encourage it in the garden by putting up enclosed nest boxes in which it will build its domed nest. It will also nest in holes in trees, buildings, banks or old sacking. Being so tiny, keeping warm is one of the wrens' biggest problems and they often suffer heavy losses in hard winters, although they are sometimes known to huddle together in nest boxes to keep warm.

Blue Tit

Parus caeruleus

Length 11.5 cm (4½ in)

The only small resident British bird with mainly blue and yellow plumage, the blue tit has yellow underparts and a blue crown, wings and tail. Its cheeks are white with a stripe around the eye, and it has a short, sturdy bill and short, round wings. The young are paler with yellower cheeks. You can encourage blue tits, as well as all the other tit species, by hanging up baskets of nuts, scraps and fat, halved coconuts and pieces of suet and fat. Like the great tit, this bird will raid milk bottles on doorsteps for the cream. Blue tits eat many garden insect pests, but they also damage buds and ripe fruit. An adaptable bid, it nests in tree holes, wall cavities and drain pipes. It likes to build in enclosed nest boxes with a 2.5–2.75 cm (1–1⅛ in) diameter entry hole and will normally lay between eight and fifteen eggs. There is nothing more rewarding than watching one youngster after another taking off from the nest box for their first flight. Blue tits do not have as distinctive or varied a range of calls as great tits, but their alarm call is a churring sound followed by a 'tsee'.

Great Tit

Parus major

Length 14 cm (5½ in)

Resident in Britain, the great tit is one of our most common garden birds and is the largest European tit. Like the blue tit, it has yellow underparts and blue-green upper parts, but it has a black crown and chin, white cheeks and a black stripe down the centre of the belly, which is wider in the male than the female. The young are paler with slightly yellow cheeks. Its bill is short and strong, and its song is a distinctive 'teacher, teacher, teacher'. A frequent visitor to bird tables and hanging nut containers, it also spends a lot of time feeding on or near the ground. It is an acrobatic species that will delight you with its antics as it hangs on halved coconuts, pieces of fat and suet, peanut baskets and bags containing scraps. It naturally nests in tree holes or wall cavities, but you can encourage it to nest by putting up an enclosed nest box with a 2.75 cm (1⅛ in) diameter entry hole and an interior depth of at least 12.5 cm (5 in).

Coal Tit

Parus ater

Length 11.5 cm (4½ in)

This active little bird of the open woodland, which particularly likes gardens where there are coniferous trees, does not visit the bird table as often as great tits and blue tits, but likes to swing on peanut containers, chunks of fat and suet and halved coconuts. In winter it is often seen foraging for spiders and insects with other tit species. Look for the white spot on the back of the fairly large blue-black head, grey upper parts and yellowish breast, and white cheeks. The young have paler underparts and yellowish cheeks. Its small size is also distinctive as it is the smallest European tit. It nests in tree holes and wall cavities but will use the same type of nest box as a blue tit. Usually single-brooded, it has seven to 11 young. It has a piping song.

Marsh Tit

Parus palustris

Length 11.5 cm (4½ in)

The name of the marsh tit is rather misleading as it is a bird of open woodland, although it is often seen in gardens. Look for its glossy black cap and chin patch, white cheeks, grey back and pale underparts. It hunts in gardens for insects, and you can attract it to the bird table and hanging containers by putting out a plentiful supply of fat and nuts. It also likes seeds, especially sunflower seeds, which it sometimes hides among moss or leaves, probably to protect them from more dominant tits. It nests in tree and wall holes and often rears two broods. It chooses enclosed nest boxes, like other tits, and you may be lucky enough to have a nesting pair using a hole in an old tree.

Long-tailed Tit

Aegithalos caudatus

Length 14 cm (5½ in)

A pretty little black, white and pink bird with a broad, dark stripe over the eye and a tail that is longer than its body, the long-tailed tit is really an inhabitant of woodland and scrub but sometimes enters gardens in winter with mixed flocks of tits and goldcrests. The young have dark cheeks. In the coldest weather it comes to bird tables and containers of fat and nuts, but usually feeds off the ground. It likes insects, berries and soft fruits, and will eat a few seeds. It has been reported more frequently in gardens in recent years as much of its natural cover in the countryside is being destroyed by farming operations. Occasionally, a pair will stay to nest in a large garden with a wild patch of scrub and brambles. The beautiful domed structure is made of cobwebs, lichens and mosses lined with thousands of feathers.

Pied Wagtail

Motacilla alba

Length 18 cm (7 in)

A small black and white bird with a long tail, the pied wagtail has a white face and chest, with black upper parts and throat, and its long tail is white on the outer edges. The female is less strongly marked and the juvenile is more browny-grey. It often runs about on garden lawns picking up insects and bobbing its tail up and down. It is also known as the dishwasher as it paddles in shallow water, including garden pools, to feed on flies and gnats. It feeds on insects and flies, and sometimes comes to garden feeding stations in winter for crumbs and household scraps. It nests in holes in walls, thatch and creepers and will occupy a ledge-type or open-fronted wooden nest box, which must be fixed to a wall or placed in a cavity that is safe from prowling cats.

Goldcrest

Regulus regulus

Length 9 cm (3½ in)

Britain's tiniest bird, weighing a mere 5 g, the goldcrest likes gardens and woods where there are coniferous and evergreen trees, spending much of its time flitting among the branches or searching bark for insects, spiders and larvae. It can be easily recognised by its small size, dull green back and orange-yellow crest bordered with black, which develops on maturity; the crown of the female is slightly lighter in colour. It mixes with flocks of tits and treecreepers in winter. It is very tame and comes to bird tables to peck at fat or to eat small crumbs. Highly acrobatic, the goldcrest is lively and fearless, and makes up in pugnacity for what it lacks in size. Its nest is an intricately woven hammock of spiders' webs and moss hung from a branch of a coniferous tree.

Siskin

Carduelis spinus

Length 12 cm (4¾ in)

This delightful little finch has advanced because of the spread of conifer plantations and is often to be seen in gardens. Green and yellow with dark wings with a yellow bar across, the male has a black crown and small black chin patch. The female does not have the black head, and is more a heavily streaked grey-green, while the juvenile is streaked and greenish-brown. The siskin is particularly attracted to peanuts hung up in red nylon-mesh bags, although no one knows exactly why it is so fond of the red colour, and it will sometimes come to bird tables for seeds and nuts. In winter it flocks with redpoll and feeds on the seeds of silver birch and alder, clinging acrobatically to the tiny cones. In summer it disperses to nest in northern coniferous woodland.

Nuthatch

Sitta europaea

Length 14 cm (5½ in)

A tree-climbing woodland bird with a powerful pointed bill like that of a woodpecker, the nuthatch is a beautiful little blue-grey bird with a pinky-yellow underside. It has a short tail and strong legs and claws, well adapted for its woodland habitat, and often moves head-downwards on tree trunks or branches. A favourite visitor to bird tables and containers of nuts and fat because of its quick and acrobatic habits, it wedges nuts and acorns in crevices in trees and batters them open. Put out sunflower seeds, peanuts, fat and cake for it on the bird table. It normally nests in a tree hole – favourite trees being oak and ash – but you can sometimes encourage it to occupy an enclosed nest box. It makes its nest of loose pieces of bark. The female reduces the entry hole with mud to make it just the right size.

Treecreeper

Certhia familiaris

Length 13 cm (5 in)

This small woodland bird creeps up trees and branches in a mouse-like way, moving in a series of jerks and pressing its long stiff tail against the bark for support. It has mottled brown plumage with a white breast and rusty-coloured rump, and its bill is sharp and gently curved. If you have a Wellingtonia tree in the garden you are likely to find a treecreeper roosting in an egg-shaped hollow that it has excavated in the soft bark with its long bill. It does not come to bird tables but you can attract it into the garden by putting crushed nuts and porridge in tree crevices. It sometimes uses a conventional enclosed nest box, but it prefers a special wedge-shaped box or a piece of bark or cork nailed to a tree. It has a loud, high-pitched call.

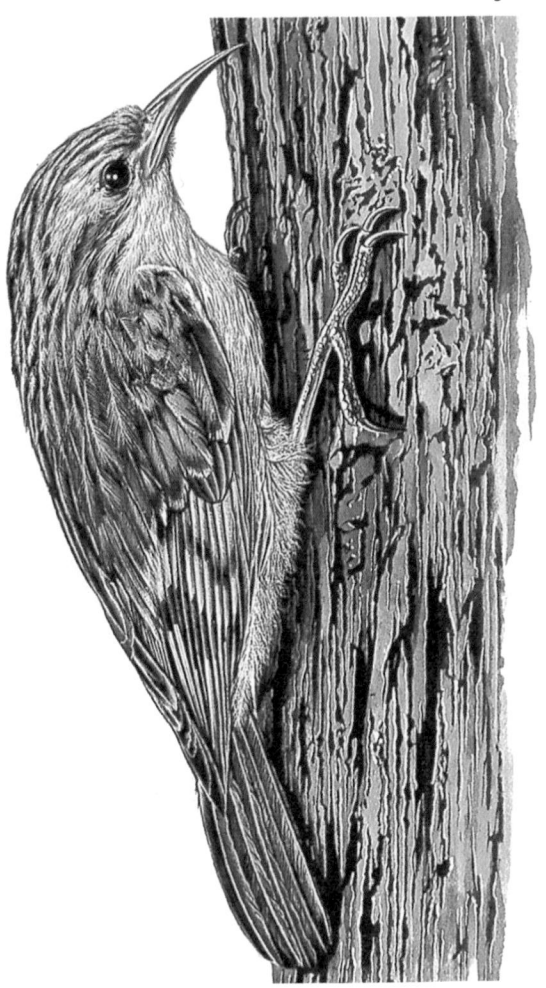

Spotted Flycatcher

Muscicapa striata

Length 14 cm (5½ in)

A summer visitor from Africa, this slim, grey-brown bird has large dark eyes and streaky plumage, paler on the underparts. It is a wonderful flier, dashing out from a perch to snap up passing insects as large as dragonflies and butterflies. It nests against walls or tree trunks, or in holes of trees and walls, making a loose cup of rootlets, moss, twigs and feathers, but you can encourage it to nest in the garden by putting up an open-fronted wooden nest box, as long as you make sure that it is in a protected site not accessible to cats. A creature of habit, the spotted flycatcher returns year after year to a favourite nest site. Spotted flycatchers like wooden posts or dead branches from which to make their insect-catching flights and you can put up a post with a crosspiece for them in the garden.

Blackcap

Sylvia atricapilla

Length 14 cm (5½ in)

This warbler is a summer visitor to the garden from Africa, although some do winter in Britain and are often seen at bird tables. You can tell the male from the female by his glossy cap – the hen and the juvenile have a reddish-brown crown – topping the grey-brown plumage on the back and pale breast. The blackcap keeps well hidden for most of the time, but in autumn and winter ventures out to feed on crumbs, scraps, rolled oats and berries on the bird table, and the glossy red berries of the honeysuckle. Blackberries and soft fruits are also favourite foods. It eats large quantities of harmful insects, so is likely to be popular with the gardener. A fine singer, it is considered by some to be second only to the nightingale.

Chaffinch

Fringilla coelebs

Length 15 cm (6 in)

The most common British finch, the chaffinch comes regularly to bird tables and ground feeding stations from its main habitat in woodland. It likes all kinds of seeds, bird pudding, scraps and berries. If you have well-grown beech trees in the garden, look for flocks of chaffinches feeding on the fallen beechmast. The male has a beautiful pinkish-russet breast, russet cheeks and back, a grey-blue crown and dark wings and tail with white bars. The female is less showy, with her greenish-brown upper parts and grey-brown chest, although she also shows the distinctive white bars on the wings and the edges of the tail. British birds are joined in winter by flocks from the Continent. It nests in old fruit trees, hedges and wall shrubs. The nest is one of the most beautiful built by a British bird. Lichens, grass and spiders' webs are used in its construction.

Bullfinch

Pyrrhula pyrrhula

Length 14.5 cm (5¾ in)

If you are a keen gardener or fruit grower you will view this handsome bird with very mixed feelings. It eats many buds of fruit trees and ornamental shrubs, but it does also eat a lot of weed seeds, including nettle and dock. It occasionally visits bird tables for seeds but prefers to forage for wild and garden seeds and berries. It is particularly fond of blackberries, privet berries and honeysuckle berries. The male is quite unmistakable, with its salmon-pink underparts, blue-grey back, black head, tail and wings, and white rump. The female is a much more subtle grey-brown, while the young are brown and do not have the distinctive black cap. It is a plump bird with a short, strong bill. It nests in thick evergreens and hedges.

Greenfinch

Carduelis chloris

Length 14.5 cm (5¾ in)

A plump, strong-billed garden bird that is increasing in numbers, the greenfinch adores peanuts and is often the dominant bird at hanging nut containers. It comes to bird tables for all kinds of seeds, buckwheat and shelled nuts. If you have a rose hedge or bushes, greenfinches will come to eat the hips in winter. The male greenfinch is a handsome bird with his olive-green plumage and bright yellow flashes on wings and tail; his mate is greyer and duller with less prominent yellow flashes. The young are less distinctively marked and more streaked. Greenfinches are sociable and nest in groups of two to six pairs, making a robust nest of grass, moss and lichen lined with hair and feathers. The male makes bat-like song flights with slowly flapping wings.

Goldfinch

Carduelis carduelis

Length 12 cm (4¾ in)

This beautiful bird has a song that is as bright as its colouring. The stripe of gold on the black wing is common both to adults and young, as is the subtle pinky-brown back, pale chest and black tail with white spots. Only the adults have the distinctive red face, and white and black striped head. It commonly enters gardens to eat seeds with its sturdy, pointed bill and to nest in fruit trees, hedges and evergreen bushes. It will come to bird tables for mixed seeds, but it prefers to forage for the seeds in garden plants and weeds, especially thistles and teasels. Leave some of your garden bedding and border plants, such as gaillardia, cosmos and french marigold, as goldfinches like to feed on the seed heads in autumn. The goldfinch's elegant cup-shaped nest of mosses, grasses and lichens is often built in garden fruit trees or espalier bushes trained against walls.

Hawfinch

Coccothraustes coccothraustes

Length 18 cm (7 in)

A shy bird normally found in woods and parks or old orchards, the hawfinch will sometimes come into gardens. It is a wary visitor to the bird table for nuts, fruits and seeds. It has a massive bill, which it uses to crack open cherry and plum stones to get at the kernels, and is a relatively large finch with a heavy body. In summer it comes into the garden to eat garden peas. Easily identified by its top-heavy look accentuated by its short tail, it has an orange head with a grey stripe around the neck, pinkish-brown underparts, a white rump and shoulder patches, and black wings. The female is slightly duller, and the young are yellow-brown. It nests on horizontal boughs of fruit trees. You can encourage it into the garden by planting cherry and plum trees, or hornbeam trees as it is fond of the winged seeds of the hornbeam.

Brambling

Fringilla montifringilla

Length 14.5 cm (5¾ in)

A close relative of the chaffinch, the brambling comes to Britain in winter from Scandinavia. In cold weather it visits bird tables with chaffinches for the mixed seeds and is particularly fond of buckwheat, hemp and millet. It feeds in the wild on beechmast and seeds scattered on the ground. Look for the male brambling's orange-buff breast and shoulders, and his black back head and bill in the breeding season; he loses much of the black in winter. The female is duller and more grey, but both sexes have conspicuous white rumps. They call with a harsh 'dwee' note, rather like that of the greenfinch.

Reed Bunting

Emberiza schoeniclus

Length 15 cm (6 in)

Like its cousin the yellowhammer, the reed bunting is an increasingly common visitor to British gardens in winter, and many stay all the year round. It normally lives in marshy and reedy places, but moves into suburban areas when the weather becomes harsh in search of mixed seeds and crumbs put out on bird tables. The male reed bunting is also known as the reed sparrow because of its brown back and dark head markings. Its black head contrasts with a white moustache streak. Females and young birds are streaky brown with a black and white moustache and lack the black head markings.

Yellowhammer

Emberiza citrinella

Length 16.5 cm (6½ in)

With its yellow head, slim body and yellow-brown rump, the yellowhammer, or yellow bunting, has white feathers on the outside of its tail that can be seen when it is in flight. The male is distinguished from the female by a more lemon-yellow head and underparts and a chestnut rump; the female is less yellow with dark streaks on the head and throat. Its song is the traditional 'little-bit-of-bread-and-no-cheese', although in Scotland it is sometimes rendered as 'may the devil take you'. Yellowhammers generally live in open countryside with hedgerows or patches of woodland, and build their nests of dried grasses lined with finer grass and hair, hiding them well on the ground, in a bank or hedge, in ivy or on a wall. They feed largely on seeds of weeds, with some grain and wild fruit, as well as insects and small ground animals. In winter they are gregarious and will often tend to flock with other seed-eating birds.

Waxwing

Bombycilla garrulus

Length 19 cm (7½ in)

A highly sociable and often tame bird, the waxwing has a call that is a soft trilling 'sirrr', which it will repeat frequently. Easily recognisable by its unmistakable pinkish-chestnut crest and short, yellow-tipped tail, it has black eye-stripes and a black throat patch. Its upper parts are chestnut, and it has a grey rump. The wings are dark and boldly marked white and yellow, with scarlet, waxy tips to the secondaries, which are less evident on the female. The favourite food of the waxwing is the rowan berry but they will also eat cotoneaster, pyracantha, viburnum, juniper, hips and haws. It often turns up in parks and gardens in the winter to gorge on the berries of ornamental trees and shrubs. Waxwings do not nest in Britain, preferring to breed in Scandinavia.

House Martin

Delichon urbica

Length 12.5 cm (5 in)

A summer visitor, the house martin nests in groups under roofs and eaves of houses. Two, sometimes three, broods are reared in mud-cup nests. It differs from the swallow in having a white rump patch that contrasts with its blue-black upper parts and white underparts. Its tail is not as deeply forked as the swallow's and the swallow has a chestnut forehead and throat. If you want to attract house martins, you can put up artificial nests under the eaves or high window sills. House martins eat large numbers of flying insects, feeding almost entirely on the wing, and for this reason you should make a special effort to encourage them to nest.

Swift

Apus apus

Length 16.5 cm (6½ in)

Perhaps more than any other sight or sound, the screaming squadrons of swifts that fill the sky for a few short months symbolise the English summer. Its screaming call has led to its being know in parts of England as the devil bird. Swifts feed, drink, sleep and even mate on wing, sometimes staying aloft for several weeks outside the breeding season. They are sociable birds, often flying in tight flocks. They feed on flying insects and wing-borne spiders, and may consume up to 50 g (2 oz) of these in a day. The swift is one of the latest migrants to arrive in Britain and one of the earliest to leave. They mate for life and the sexes are alike, with black-brown plumage, except for a white chin-patch, which is seldom visible. Special swift nest boxes are available.

Swallow

Hirundo rustica

Length 19 cm (7½ in)

A summer visitor to house and garden that spends the winter in southern Africa, the swallow builds an open, cup-shaped mud nest on beams and ledges or against walls. It often chooses porches and outhouses in which to rear its young, and there are usually two broods. You can encourage swallows to nest by putting up a shallow wooden tray, or half a coconut, on a joist or rafter. They will also use the artificial nests made for house martins if they are specially adapted and put up singly inside buildings. Swallows catch insects on the wing, from ground level to as high as 150 metres (500 ft). They are easily recognisable by their long tail, red-brown chin and forehead and bottle-blue rump, which stands out against dark wings and back. They have a dark chest band and a pinkish-white belly. The young are less brightly coloured with shorter tails.

Jackdaw

Corvus monedula

Length 33 cm (13 in)

A small member of the crow family, the jackdaw is the only black bird with a grey nape and ear coverts. They live in groups and frequently come into gardens, attracted by bird tables where they eat scraps, cold potatoes, fruit, berries and nuts. They also eat mixed scraps put down on the ground. Seeds and small invertebrates are part of their natural diet. In spring, jackdaws can be a menace because they eat the eggs and young of other birds, and they build stick nests in chimneys, sometimes blocking them. If you want to have nesting jackdaws in the garden, you can put up open-fronted nest boxes, or enclosed-type boxes with an entry hole of not less than 15 cm (6 in) in diameter.

Carrion Crow

Corvus corone corone

Length 47 cm (18½ in)

A notorious egg thief, the carrion crow has also discovered a way of smashing open shells by dropping them from a height, a habit that suggests, like the rest of the crow family, it is a quick learner. One of its call notes sounds strangely like a motor-horn, but its main call is a hoarse 'kack', usually uttered three times in succession. A carrion crow has a powerful bill, all-black plumage and a square tail. It can be distinguished from an adult rook by the fact that the base of the bill is fully feathered and it lacks the feathered 'trousers' of the rook. Also it does not spread its wing feathers as much as a rook in flight. Crows are also less sociable birds and are more likely to be seen on their own. They eat grains, seeds, insects, wild fruit, snails and sometimes small mammals.

Rook

Corvus frugilegus

Length 46 cm (18 in)

This black bird can easily be confused with the carrion crow, but has a steeper forehead and a more slender and more pointed greyish-white bill. Its chest and leg feathers tend to be loose, so it looks as though it is wearing short trousers. Rooks are among the most sociable of birds and tend to nest in colonies, but prefer agricultural areas and are not often attracted to anything but the largest of gardens. They are also prone to stealing and will often take sticks from the nests of neighbouring pairs while the rightful owners are away collecting more nesting material.

Magpie

Pica pica

Length 46 cm (18 in)

This large and long-tailed bird hunts on the ground and in hedges for small animals, birds and insects and it is also fond of fruit, nuts, peas and berries. It raids the nests of garden birds to take and eat eggs and young. Magpies are liable to hide not only surplus food but also any colourful or shiny objects that take their fancy. In autumn and winter it will visit bird tables or garden ground feeding stations for household scraps, which it usually takes away to eat. Like the jackdaw, this is a fierce predator of other birds so it is not always welcome in the garden. Its plumage is a striking black and white, with a greenish sheen on the tail, and it is often seen in pairs or small groups. It nests mainly in woodland, making a large, domed nest of mud, twigs, feathers and softer material surrounded by sticks.

Jay

Garrulus glandarius

Length 34 cm (13½ in)

If you have a large garden with plenty of trees you are certain to receive a visit from this unmistakable woodland bird. It is fond of acorns, which it buries for winter food, and will come to bird tables and ground feeding areas for household scraps, cold potatoes, corn, beechmast, nuts, fruit and berries. Do not encourage too many visits from jays as they are serious predators of eggs and young birds in the garden. They are particularly partial to green peas, an annoying habit that puts them on the gardener's 'black list'. Look for the white rump and bright blue and black wing patches, which show up in flight. The bird has a beautiful pinkish-brown body and a black moustache.

Green Woodpecker

Picus viridis

Length 32 cm (12½ in)

This woodland bird, the largest and most colourful of British woodpeckers, has dark green wings with black and white markings, and a paler green-yellow front and neck. The crown is red and the face black with a black moustache, the male having a red edge to his moustache. In flight, look for the conspicuous yellow rump. The bird will come into gardens to feed on the ants' nests in lawns or trees, picking up the ants and their pupae with its long, sticky tongue, which can protrude up to 10 cm (4 in) out of its sharp, strong beak. It likes to search for insect larvae in three trunks and branches, pressing against the surface with its stiff tail for balance, and using its zygodactyl feet (two toes pointing forward, two backward) to make it an agile mover. It sometimes visits bird tables in winter for bird pudding, mealworms and fat. Normally the green woodpecker bores its own nest hole in trees, but it can be encouraged to nest in gardens with large trees by putting up an enclosed nest box with a 6.5 cm (2½ in) diameter entrance hole and a depth of 39 cm (15 in). It is sometimes called the yaffle because its loud ringing call can sound almost like laughter.

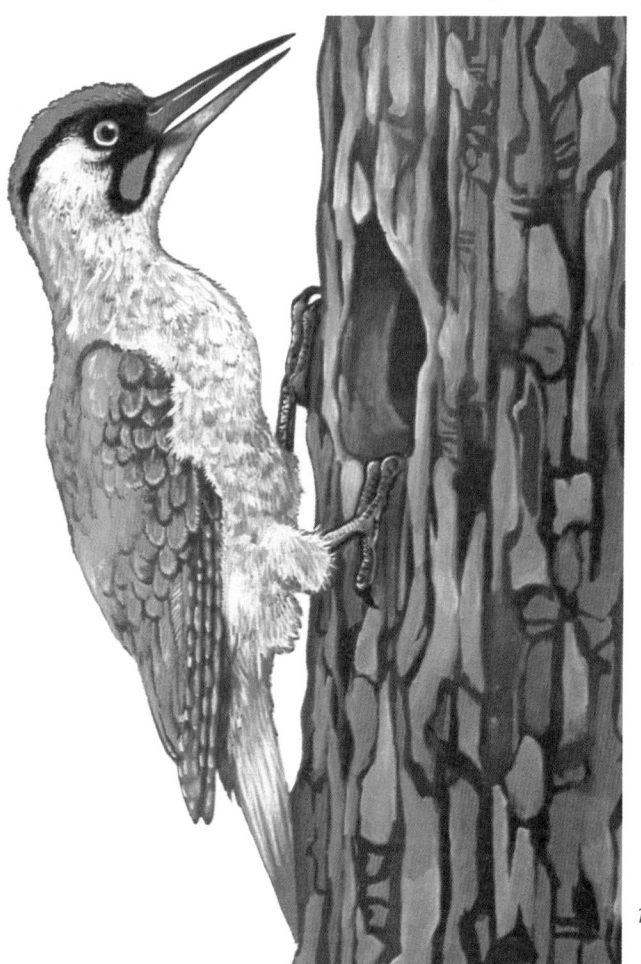

Great Spotted Woodpecker

Dendrocopos major

Length 23 cm (9 in)

The great spotted woodpecker is the commonest British woodpecker and is found in large gardens with well-grown trees, as well as in woods and parks. It hammers trees and dead wood for insects and larvae with its strong, sharp bill, and wedges nuts in crevices to crack them open. It picks up insects with its long, barbed tongue. You can attract it to bird tables by putting out suet, fat and nuts. It is as agile as tits in hanging upside-down on a piece of suet and, unlike the green woodpecker, it is seldom seen on the ground. As well as excavating its own nest hole in a tree, it will use an enclosed nest box with a 5 cm (2 in) diameter entry hole and an interior depth of 30 cm (12 in). It has striking black and white plumage with a bright red rump, and a smaller, slightly plumper body than the green woodpecker. The male also has a patch of bright red on the back of his head but the female has a black crown. The young all have completely red crowns.

Wood Pigeon

Columba palumbus
Length 41 cm (16 in)

The largest and most common pigeon, this is also known as the ring dove because of the white ring on its neck, which also has distinctive glossy green and purple colouring. Look for the white bars on its wings, which are visible in flight, pinkish chest and dark bar on the tail. It has a longer tail than the feral pigeon. Its wings make a noisy clatter when it takes off. This is not a popular visitor to gardens as it will greedily eat green crops such as cabbages, Brussels sprouts and kale, particularly in hard winter weather. In summer, it raids rows of garden peas. It comes to garden feeding stations and is fond of grain and large seeds. Although mainly a ground feeder, the wood pigeon occasionally visits bird tables for bread, household scraps and seeds. The song is the well-known cooing phrase, usually made up of five notes, 'cooooo-coo, coo-coo, coo'.

Feral Pigeon

Columba livia

Length 33 cm (13 in)

More of a town-garden bird, the feral pigeon tends to live in city squares, docks and railway stations, where it will even snatch scraps from people's plates. Its survival has been due mainly to the amount of food – such as bread, cake and bird seed – offered by the public, especially in the winter. The cooing voice of the feral pigeon is a familiar sound in cities. Its original ancestors were the domestic pigeons that escaped from medieval dovecotes. Its plumage tends to vary in colour far more than other varieties of pigeon, ranging from rusty-brown to blue-grey or even white. It also tends to be slightly smaller than the wood pigeon.

Collared Dove

Streptopelia decaocto

Length 32 cm (12½ in)

This attractive dove first arrived in Britain in the early 1950s, after spreading across the Continent from Asia, and is now common in gardens. It often feeds in chicken runs and regularly comes to bird tables and ground feeding stations for seeds, grains, peas and scraps. It also likes young foliage and berries. Look for its ash-brown plumage, with black half collar edged with white, and its dark wing tips. It likes perching on TV aerials where it sings with a treble-noted 'coo', which has the accent on the second syllable. It nests on a platform, usually in a coniferous tree, and raises several broods between March and October.

Stock Dove

Columba oenas

Length 33 cm (13 in)

Rather small and darker than the wood pigeon, the stock dove has a gruff voice – a coughing or double grunting – that is very different from the wood pigeon's cooing. Its upper parts are blue-grey, with a glossy green patch on the side of the neck, and it has only small wing bars. The behaviour of the stock dove is very much like that of a wood pigeon. Stock doves are social birds and tend to breed in loose colonies, but territorial disputes can break out between males. They eat the seeds of weeds and grains, and some animal food, especially cocoons of earthworms. They will nest in holes in trees, on buildings, in rabbit burrows and nest boxes, as well as in holes in cliffs and sand-dunes.

Tawny Owl

Strix aluco

Length 38 cm (15 in)

Also known as the brown owl or wood owl this beneficial bird, the most common British owl, hunts for rodents in large gardens, parks and woodlands, and is not uncommon in the centre of some towns or villages. As well as eating rats and mice, it also feeds on small birds, insects, worms and even frogs and newts, hunting mainly at night. It can be attracted to gardens with large mature trees by putting up an enclosed chimney-type nest box with a 20 cm (8 in) diameter entry hole at the top and an inside depth of 76 cm (30 in); the floor should be 20 cm (8 in) square. Tawny owls will also nest in old wooden barrels if holes are cut in them and the barrels are placed in the forks of trees well above the ground. More often heard than seen, the male gives out his eerie 'hooo, hooo, hoo-oo-oo', with the female replying with a sharp 'kee-wick'. The plumage is mottled brown, the upperparts varying from warm brown to tawny or greyish. It has a large round head and a stocky body, dark eyes and fairly broad wings on which it takes long glides from its favoured perching posts.

Black-headed Gull

Larus ridibundus

Length 38 cm (15 in)

Black-headed gulls moved up from the Thames estuary during hard winters at the end of the nineteenth century, finding food around the docks, in parks and along embankments where people threw scraps. A scavenger by nature, it is more common inland during the harsh and stormy weather of winter, and is the commonest gull to be seen inland, most often in parks or rubbish tips, although it will visit gardens, especially early in the year. It is one of the smaller gulls and can be recognised by its grey back and wings, black wing-tips and white plumage, and red feet and bill. Its wings are narrow and pointed with a dark trailing edge. In the breeding season, it has a dark chocolate-brown hood, which does not extend down on to the neck, and it is the only big gull to show this feature. It also has a white crescent around the eye. Its winter plumage does not include the dark head, but just a dark patch over the ears.

Chapter 6
Predators, Pests and Poisons

s well as making your garden attractive to birds, it is important to try to make it as safe as possible and there are many ways in which you can do that.

Cats in the bird garden

It so happens that our household pet has always been a dog, and as a keen birdwatcher I have decided not to keep a cat as a pet, even though I do like them, as there is no escaping the fact that a cat is a resourceful predator of garden birds. Even the most domesticated cat will stalk and kill both adult and young birds – that is their nature and nothing will change it. If you have a pet cat, therefore, you may want to consider a few ways to minimise the risk to the birds in your garden.

Unfortunately, the sight and presence of a cat in the garden can alarm birds and sometimes even make them leave their nests, so even if your particular pet is not a persistent killer of birds, its presence may well deter them from coming into the garden or nesting there.

There are some things you can do to reduce the chances of your cat catching and killing your garden birds. Firstly, try to keep cats indoors when birds are at their most vulnerable – at dawn and dusk, and particularly from March to July and December to January. It is also a good idea to keep your cats well fed (but not overfed) to encourage them to stay near the home and to reduce their urge to travel to other people's gardens.

You can put a bell on the cat's collar so that the noise will warn the birds and they can escape. There are also sonic collars that give out a warning signal. This is certainly better than nothing, although not totally effective. Cats are adept at moving stealthily to reduce the sound, and the bells can jam or corrode over time so that they no longer ring, making it important that you check them regularly and replace them when necessary.

Intelligent bird gardening can help, too. Avoid putting food for birds on the ground, and place the bird tables and baths away from trees or surfaces from which a cat could jump. Use a slippery pole to support a bird table, or put an upturned tin at the base to deter the cat. Provide a range of native plants – especially thick, bushy or prickly shrubs – that provide cover for the birds when they are roosting or nesting.

If you do not have a cat but want to deter neighbours' cats from entering your garden, there are a few measures you can take. Because my dog is a boisterous cat chaser, I do not have to worry unduly about the problem, although buying a dog as your own solution should be carefully thought through!

Although not particularly attractive, a wire fence offers some defence and some of my neighbours have erected 5 cm (2 in) mesh wire netting up to 4 metres (12 ft) high. They grow climbing plants like clematis, honeysuckle and passion flower up the netting. Thick prickly hedges make good cat deterrents. Holly, hawthorn and sweet-briar are excellent, but to make sure that cats and other undesirables do not find their way through, plug any gaps with thorny cuttings. While cats can leap walls and fences as high as about 2 metres (6 ft), a length of wire netting about 50 cm (20 in) wide along the top of a fence will stop them getting over or sitting on the top. Also, the smoother the wall or fence, the more difficult it is for them to climb. You can prevent cats from climbing small trees by putting a circle of wire netting round the trunk.

You can also buy scented pellets that you can hang at particular points cats use to gain access to your garden, changing them regularly to make sure they remain effective. These are not scientifically proven to be effective but some people find them useful.

Rats, squirrels, foxes and predatory birds

Rats are a menace to the bird gardener. They will be attracted into the garden by surplus food left on the ground, or by the presence of eggs and nestlings. They are agile climbers and can scale trees and hedges in search of food. Always make sure you clean your bird table at the end of the day, and avoid putting food on the ground if you are aware of the presence of rats. If you see them in the garden, you can call in the local council's pest controller, whose details you will find in the telephone directory or Yellow Pages. If you put down rat poison yourself, the best to use are Warfarin and Raticate. Follow the instructions carefully about where to place the poison, putting it inside a section of old drainpipe to prevent other creatures from eating it by mistake.

Though the long tail and graceful movements make them far more attractive to most people, squirrels are related to rats and are equally unwelcome in the bird garden as they eat large numbers of eggs and young birds. They can even enlarge the entry holes of nest boxes to get at nestlings, so it is worth protecting nest box holes with a piece of metal. Dogs help to chase away squirrels but there are no other methods of control that are appropriate in the garden. Again, make sure that you do not encourage them near the house by leaving out scraps on the bird table or the ground, and put an upturned tin beneath your bird table.

Foxes can also be a problem, and as the urban fox population rises, this is no longer confined to the countryside. They are very much on the increase in suburban and even urban areas and are growing bolder in their raids on chickens, pet rabbits, birds' eggs and young birds. They also take food from dustbins. Since they are agile climbers, little short of an expensive, tall fox-proof wire fence will keep them out at night. You can try leaving out metal objects so that the animal might think they are traps. Clear up bird food and make sure rubbish is secure inside a dustbin with a tight-fitting lid.

There is little you can do to stop raids by jays, magpies and crows, however exasperating. Most of us are resigned to the fact that they will take a share of eggs and young birds each spring.

Pesticides and pollutants

Certain garden and agricultural pesticides and insecticides pose a threat to bird life, though in recent years special efforts have been made by manufacturers to produce chemicals that are non-toxic to animals and birds and not residual in the soil, so it is worth checking the labels before you make your purchase. Make sure you always adhere strictly to the instructions on whatever product you buy.

If you are unsure about the use of any product, then seek advice from the manufacturer. In my garden, I use only pyrethrum-based insecticides containing a substance extracted from an African-grown flower and harmless to wildlife and humans, though effective against insect pests. When using a pyrethrum spray, confine your operations to the evening when bees are off the wing.

Forget trying to eradicate slugs and snails from your garden. Without slugs and snails, you would not have many of the birds and wildlife – thrushes and hedgehogs, for example – that are such enjoyable and entertaining visitors. Concentrate instead on protecting vulnerable plants from slug attack. You can obtain a fact sheet from the RSPB about controlling slugs and snails.

Chapter 7
Projects for the Bird Gardener

When you have established your bird garden, you may want to keep a permanent record of the resident and migratory species seen throughout the year. To start with, you may want to become involved in the RSPB's Big Annual Birdwatch, and you will find details of that on page 195. There are also a number of simple projects that can widen your interest and enjoyment and add to the general store of natural history knowledge, but before I move on to those, let us consider the topic of binoculars and telescopes.

Binoculars and telescopes

I have already made some suggestions about placing the bird table and other items of bird furniture in your garden to give you the best natural view of the birds' activity without disturbing them. If your bird table and feeding containers are well positioned to give clear and reasonably close views from the house, you will certainly not need the help of the high-powered optical aids used by birdwatchers in open country or by seashore and estuary.

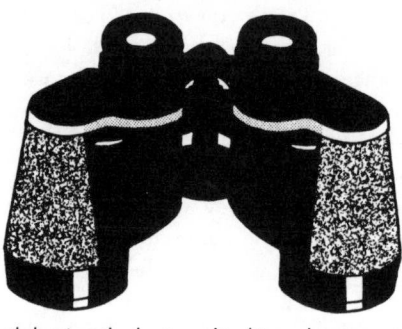

It is worth buying the best quality binoculars you can afford.

Having said that, if you have a pair of suitable, lightweight binoculars, you can watch your birds much more closely, and observe the wonderful detail of their plumage and the specifics of their behaviour.

There are three main optical points to consider when choosing to buy a pair of binoculars: magnification, field of view (usually measured in degrees, or in metres width at 1000 metres distance), and light transmission. For general birdwatching, magnifications of ×7, ×8 or ×9, with object lenses of 30 mm and 40 mm diameter are the most suitable. I use a pair of 8 × 30 binoculars for my own garden birdwatching and a pair of 10 magnification for field work.

Other things to consider are the weight of the binoculars and how they feel when you handle them. Do not be tempted to buy a pair that are too heavy for you to hold comfortably for some time, or are too large if you have small hands. There is a bewildering choice of binoculars on the market to suit all pockets, but it is a good idea to buy the best quality you can afford. If you shop at a reputable store, they will be happy to give you advice and guidance when you are making your selection. Take your time, as with care they will give a lifetime of service.

I also use a Japanese-made telescope with a fixed magnification of ×22 for watching the birds that visit my bird tables and feeders. The model I chose is compact and light and so can be used without a tripod, and the focus knob is easy to use. Again, there is a great variety so take your time, and take suitable advice, before you make your choice.

A nature diary

Keen birdwatchers keep careful notes of what they see and hear. The most common method involves using notebooks, diaries and card indexes. Years ago, when I had fewer family and business commitments, I kept a diary-style field notebook, in which I noted my daily observations of birds and other wildlife, weather conditions and all other relevant details. This method still has a lot to commend it, particularly if you have plenty of time to write up your notes and make sketches of the birds you see in the garden. Busy people may find a card index easier to keep as a source of quick reference, or you may want to keep a database on your PC.

If you decide to keep a nature diary, the first essential is a conveniently sized book with a waterproof cover. Unlined paper is preferable as this is more useful for making sketches and diagrams. Alternatively, you could choose a loose-leaf file with a plastic cover, so that you can use both lined and unlined paper, or add sketches in a particular spot at a later date.

The point of a nature diary or notebook is that you must be systematic. It is very easy to start out with a burst of enthusiasm, then get bored or lazy and stop writing. You should not make it a chore – it should be an enjoyable hobby – so start by just recording the basics and make it a good habit. You can always develop it later if you become seriously hooked. Note the date and the weather conditions, then keep a record of the species and numbers of birds you see in the garden, with notes on their behaviour and feeding habits, call notes, songs and flight patterns. If they have preferences for particular foods that you have put out or that are available in the garden, jot them down. If they appear to like feeding at the ground feeding station rather than the bird table, for example, make a note of this.

It helps if you can do a quick sketch of particular bird or an aspect of their behaviour. Having to observe them closely enough to draw them enhances your powers of observation and recollection, and you may find you see details that you had never noticed before. You can check your sketches against the photographs and information in a field guide.

Jot down all the details of the birds in a notebook or card index.

Another option is to use a simple card index for your records, and this is what I have done more recently. Index cards and a plastic box to hold them are not expensive and take up very little space. Make out a card for each species, putting its popular name in the top left-hand corner, followed by its Latin name. You can find all these details both in this book and in any reputable field guide. The scientific names are necessary because they are unique and international. If you talk about a robin with an American, for example, you would be talking about two quite different birds! The scientific name is made up of two names: the genus, the main family group, and the species, the specific type of bird. They will therefore help you understand bird families, as all the genus names of one family are the same;

for example, *Parus major* is the great tit, *Parus caeruleus* is the blue tit, *Parus ater* is the coal tit, and so on. If you make a point of writing them in your book or on your cards, you'll soon find they become familiar.

Follow the same guidelines as for the nature notebook but keep your notes concise in the limited space available. The value of a card index is ease of handling and speed of checking records. The index is also alphabetical and you don't have to wade through pages of notes to find a particular fact.

Of course you can keep all your notes on a database on your PC. If you make sketches, they can be scanned in and placed wherever you want them in the document. You can keep everything updated on screen, then print out specific information if you need it.

Sketching

Most birdwatchers make little sketches to keep with their notes, but if you enjoy sketching and painting you may want to take it a step further. Many of the greatest illustrators of natural history books began in this way. Watch the movements and postures of birds and try to capture these in preliminary sketches. Make careful notes, too, of how the natural colours strike you in changing lights. In my view, the first notebook sketches of top bird artists like Archibald Thorburn are more charming and vivacious than many of his finished paintings. They seem to me to contain the true essence of bird life.

Try your hand at painting or drawing your bird visitors.

Helping with research

As your knowledge grows, you may want to join a birdwatching organisation or to help with some of their research.

Membership of the RSPB (see page 200) brings you information, a first-class magazine, a source of fine colour films about bird life, and the chance to purchase high-quality products (although you do not have to be a member to buy bird tables and the like from them). They also offer suggestions for individual projects in the garden, as well as the chance to take part in their research surveys, such as their Big Garden Birdwatch, which takes place annually in January (see page 195).

The British Trust for Ornithology (see page 200) also produces an excellent magazine, and offers information and the chance to take part in recording projects and censuses. The data is written by amateur ornithologists on specially issued cards, analysed by computer, and the results are then published. An example is the nest box information scheme.

Bird photography

Bird photography is increasingly popular, and you can develop your skills to whatever level you wish. Simple snaps on an ordinary camera can still help in your recognition and identification if you stick them in your notebook or index or scan them into your database – or you can use a digital camera and simply transfer the images to your computer.

However, if you are keen on more serious photography, you will need to invest in better equipment and perhaps a tripod and telephoto lenses. Do not make the mistake of buying expensive equipment before you have thought through how it is going to be used and what sort of equipment you need. It is a good idea to take advice from other bird photographers on the advantages and disadvantages of various cameras or equipment, or even try them out if you can before you make your choice. Having said that, the bird gardener has plenty of splendid opportunities to photograph birds close up, or drinking, bathing and feeding.

Recording bird songs and calls

You may wish to try to record some songs or calls of the birds in your garden. Recordings of a very high quality need sophisticated and expensive equipment, but it is surprising how good results often are with some of the standard and relatively inexpensive microphones and cassette recorders. Magazines on recording often contain helpful articles for the beginner. You can also buy recorded bird songs from the RSPB and some commercial companies, which help you to identify and memorise the notes made by your garden birds.

Good results can be obtained by recording birds songs on
a basic cassette recorder.

Chapter 8
Looking After Injured Birds

From time to time you may come across an injured bird, or a fledgling that is orphaned or has prematurely left the nest. All too often, well-meaning people try to take over the care of young birds but you should think carefully before doing this as it is not necessarily the best course of action. Most young birds that venture out of the nest are still being fed by their parents and should not be moved or touched. If you do so, the parents may then, in fact, abandon them. If you have a cat, keep it out of the way for a little while until the bird goes back to safety.

Caring for young birds

If you do decide that the bird has definitely been abandoned, you should still think carefully about whether you have the considerable time and patience it requires to act as a foster parent. Read the next paragraph to get some idea of the commitment you are making; it will not be easy. If you do not have the time, it is better to destroy the bird humanely, or to hand it to someone more skilled at looking after it.

Once you have decided that you will act as a foster parent, it would still be wise to seek advice from a specialist organisation such as the RSPB. First you need to find a warm, draught-free place to keep the bird, perhaps in a cardboard box lined with newspaper but with plenty of ventilation holes. Young birds can be fed a mixture of dead flies, smooth (never hairy) caterpillars and minced raw meat from the end of a matchstick. Birds of prey need roughage such as dead mice and chicks complete with fur or feathers. Don't feed live food; kill insects beforehand. Regular feeds, hourly round the clock, are essential, and you must also provide a constant supply of clean water. As the youngster grows and begins to exercise its wings, take it into the garden, show it live caterpillars and insects and encourage it to fend for itself. It should be independent in about a month.

Only attempt to foster an orphaned bird if you have the necessary time and patience.

Injured birds

If you find an exhausted or injured bird in the garden, the first thing to do is to cover it with a colander or box that will protect it from local cats or other predators but allow it enough time to rest and recoup its energy. In most cases, you will find that once the bird has rested for a while, it will either push its way out under the colander, or will fly away as soon as you lift off the covering.

If the bird is seriously exhausted or starved, again make sure that you can commit the time to caring for it. Place it in a cardboard box lined with newspaper and punched with ventilation holes, and keep it in a warm place. Keep the top of the box in the dark so that the bird does not fly up to the light and hurt itself. Provide a shallow bowl of water, food and a stick, placed low down, for a perch. Seed-eating birds should be offered a standard seed mixture. Insect-eating or omnivorous birds needs insects, chopped worms, smooth caterpillars, finely shredded meat and some of the proprietary insect food sold by pet shops. Never give exhausted birds alcohol.

As the bird recovers, leave a light on to encourage it to eat. When it is strong enough to fly, release it back into the wild, but if its condition deteriorates, take it at once to an RSPCA clinic. You will find their information in the your local telephone book.

Seriously injured birds should be taken straight to the nearest vet, RSPCA or PDSA clinic, where they can be given expert attention.

Birds and the law

Everyone who attracts and feeds birds should become acquainted with the law as it relates to bird life. Basically, all birds and their eggs are protected under the Protection of Birds Act 1954 (with amendments in 1967), except for game birds and certain scheduled pest species, which may be killed or taken by authorised people. Game birds and pests are listed in the schedule at the end of the Act. If you want to know more about the law affecting birds you should write to the RSPB, or you can contact your nearest police station or RSPCA inspector. The RSPB publishes a useful booklet on *Birds and the Law* and will send a copy on receipt of a first-class stamp.

A box lined with newspaper will provide a safe resting place for an injured bird.

Chapter 9
The RSPB Big Garden Birdwatch

Taking an interest in the birds in your garden goes far deeper than just sheer personal enjoyment – it can be of real scientific benefit, especially to the Royal Society for the Protection of Birds. For more than two decades, the RSPB has relied heavily on the data collected once a year by ordinary people throughout Britain to assess the number of different species of garden birds in the UK and also to highlight long-term population trends.

Big Garden Birdwatch, which is organised annually by RSPB Wildlife Explorers, the junior section of the Society, is the biggest and longest-running garden bird survey in the world. Every year since one cold and snowy Saturday morning in January 1979, children and adults have recorded the maximum number of birds seen at one time in their garden over a period of one hour.

Thousands of Big Garden Birdwatch forms each year are sent to Wildlife Explorers, formerly the RSPB's Young Ornithologists' Club, and the results are counted and sorted to find the top ten birds for the England, Wales, Scotland and

Northern Ireland, and finally the top 20 garden birds in Britain. The results have provided information both interesting and vital for the ongoing welfare of our garden birds. This is because, as natural foods become less available in the wider countryside, UK gardens increasingly are proving important havens for birds and other wildlife, and the survey helps to record a clear and accurate snapshot of our many and varied feathered friends.

Numbers of familiar garden birds are declining rapidly and if the situation is to be reversed then it is vital that as much information as possible is gathered, and one way is through the Big Garden Birdwatch's annual mid-winter survey, which enables the RSPB and other wildlife organisations to take appropriate action.

Over the years, starlings and house sparrows have remained the top two birds in Britain and this was again the case in 2001. However, the survey has repeatedly shown that the average number of starlings per garden has dropped by 45 per cent over the last two decades and the average number of house sparrows by 50 per cent, thus confirming what the RSPB has suspected for some time.

The list of top ten birds for 2001 includes eight varieties that were in the original top ten in 1979. The song thrush, now eighteenth, has been replaced by the collared dove, and the dunnock (twelfth), has been replaced by the wood pigeon. The chaffinch, though showing a slight decrease in 2001, has increased 50 per cent since the survey began and collared dove numbers are up by 120 per cent. Interestingly, the blue tit jumped from fifth to third place, swapping places with the chaffinch. The robin (seventh) and the great tit (eighth) also swapped their 2000 positions.

The Big Garden Birdwatch was also one of the first surveys to show a fall in song thrush numbers in our gardens. It has now been declared a bird of high conservation concern and the RSPB is carrying out research to try and find out the reasons for its continuing decline.

Of course, bird numbers vary from year to year. More birds die in harsh winters while some summers turn out to be better breeding seasons than others. This is why scientists need to compare the figures over several years before they can be certain of any real decrease in numbers. In 1998, recorded bird numbers dropped appreciably. There were several reasons for this, but the most likely is that January that year was exceptionally mild and so birds did not need to visit gardens to find food. In 1999, it was much colder and birds visited gardens in their search for food and, therefore, numbers rose again.

Approximately 30,000 households – more than 37,000 adults and 13,000 children – were involved in the 2001 counts. Over 90 species were recorded and the survey discovered that the most unusual garden visitors were waxwings, kingfishers, lesser spotted woodpeckers, hawfinches, mandarin ducks and ring-necked parakeets. An amazing 4 per cent of gardens recorded wintering blackcaps!

The RSPB survey is carried out each year on the last weekend of January. Schools can take part on any one day during the same week. Forms can be obtained by writing to: Big Garden Birdwatch, RSPB Wildlife Explorers, The Lodge, Sandy, Bedfordshire, SG19 2DL. Instructions on how to enter can also be found on the RSPB website (www.rspb.org.uk).

RSPB 2001 garden survey

Position	Species	Average seen	Total	Position in 2000
1	Starling	4.2	121,838	1
2	House sparrow	4.0	114,984	2
3	Blue tit	3.2	91,497	5
4	Blackbird	2.8	81,117	4
5	Chaffinch	2.0	57,691	3
6	Greenfinch	1.7	48,426	6
7	Robin	1.5	42,286	8
8	Great tit	1.4	41,342	7
9	Collared dove	1.3	37,566	9
10	Wood pigeon	1.0	28,959	10

Top ten most widespread species

Species	Percentage of gardens occupied
Blackbird	87.6
Blue tit	81.5
Robin	81.0
House sparrow	62.4
Starling	56.1
Great tit	56.1
Chaffinch	54.2
Collared dove	51.5
Greenfinch	44.0
Wood pigeon	39.8

Useful Addresses

The Royal Society for the Protection of Birds (RSPB)
The Lodge, Sandy, Bedfordshire
SG19 2DL
Tel: 01767 680551
Fax: 01767 692365
Website: www.rspb.org.uk
The leading organisation for bird conservation. It owns and runs many reserves, arranges meetings and exhibitions, makes and shows colour films and publishes much illustrated literature. Quarterly magazine issued free to members, *Birds*.

Wildlife Explorers
The Lodge, Sandy, Bedfordshire
SG19 2DL
Tel: 01767 680551
Fax: 01767 692365
Website: www.rspb.org.uk
Formerly the Young Ornithologists' Club, it is the national club for young birdwatchers (ages 7 to 15). Quarterly magazine, *Bird Life*.

British Trust for Ornithology
The Nunnery, Thetford, Norfolk
IP24 2PU
Tel: 01842 750050
Fax: 01842 750030
E-mail: info@bto.org
Website: www.bto.org
Senior scientific organisation, which most serious amateur birdwatchers join. Members can take part in field studies, censuses and other systematic work. Lending library available. Two journals published three times a year, *Bird Study* and *Ringing and Migration*. Newsletter issued six times a year free to members, *BTO News*.

People's Dispensary for Sick Animals
Whitechapel Way, Priorslee, Telford, Shropshire TF2 9PQ
Tel: 01952 290999
Fax: 01952 292741
Website: www.pdsa.org.uk
A charity organisation that provides free veterinary care for sick and injured companion animals.

Royal Pigeon Racing Association

The Reddings, near Cheltenham, Gloucestershire GL51 6RN
Tel: 01452 713529
Fax: 01452 857119
E-mail: strays@rpra.org
Website: www.rpra.org
The administrative body for pigeon racing throughout the UK.

Royal Society for the Protection of Cruelty to Animals (RSPCA)

Wilberforce Way, Southwater, Horsham, West Sussex
RH13 9RS
Tel: 0870 333 5999
Website: www.rspca.org.uk
The major UK organisation aims to prevent cruelty to animals of all kinds.

Scottish Ornithologists' Club

21 Regent Terrace, Edinburgh
EH7 5BT Scotland
Tel: 0131 556 6042
Fax: 0131 558 9947
E-mail: mail@the-soc.org.uk
Website: www.the-soc.org.uk
The major organisation for ornithology in Scotland.

Equipment suppliers

RSPB

(Address see facing page.)
Range of equipment.

C.J. Wildbird Foods

The Rea, Upton Magna, Shrewsbury, Shropshire
SY4 4UR
Tel: 0800 731 2820
Fax: 01743 709504
E-mail: enquiries@birdfood.co.uk
Website: www.birdfood.co.uk
Bird food, feeders, variety of nest boxes, water baths.

Gardman Ltd

High Street, Moulton, Lincolnshire PE12 6QD
Tel: 01406 372222
Fax: 01406 372233
E-mail: sales@gardman.co.uk
Website: www.gardman.co.uk
Manufacturers of huge range of wild bird food and other products.

Jamie Wood Products
1 Green Street, Old Town,
Eastbourne, East Sussex
BN21 1QN
Tel/Fax: 01323 727291
E-mail:
jamiewood@birdtables.com
Website: www.birdtables.com
Bird tables, nest boxes and other
equipment.

Jacobi Jayne & Co.
Wealden Forest Park,
Herne Common, Canterbury,
Kent CT6 7LQ
Tel: 01227 714314
Fax: 01227 719235
E-mail:
enquries@jacobijayne.com
Website: www.jacobijayne.com
Range of high-quality bird
feeders, nest boxes, bird foods
and accessories. Wildlife tip
sheets available free of charge.

**Scottish National Institution
for the War Blinded**
Linburn Workshop, Wilkieston
by Kirknewton, Midlothian
EH27 8DU
Tel: 0131 333 1369
Fax: 0131 333 4841
Various nest boxes. Leaflets
available on request.

Index